THE COMPLETE
SLOW
COOKER
COOKBOOK

THE COMPLETE SLOW COOKER COOKBOOK

75 tasty, time-saving, slow-cooked recipes

CONTENTS

6 A GUIDE TO SLOW COOKING

12 EASY WEEKNIGHTS

48 CURRIES, SOUPS & STEWS

84 DINNER PARTY DISHES

116 BATCH COOKING

146 DESSERTS

172 INDEX

A GUIDE TO SLOW COOKING

PREP, SET, AND FORGET

Slow cooking is one of the simplest ways to create amazing meals with loads of flavour. Heart-warming family favourites like stews, soups, and curries all benefit from long, slow cooking. But what families love most about this method of cooking is how effortless it is for the cook. The cooking time might be slow, but the prep time is fast! It should take less than 30 minutes to get your ingredients sorted and in the cooker. Then it's just a matter of setting the time and letting the appliance do the rest.

As straightforward as most slow cooking recipes are, it is best not to just throw all your ingredients in. That's where the prep comes in. In most cases, we've kept to around 15 minutes to get your ingredients ready, which includes any frying or heating in a pan on the stove before it goes in the appliance for its set cooking time.

Most of your favourite soup, stew, tagine, and curry recipes are suitable for use in a slow cooker. You may need to adjust the liquid content to accommodate the long, slow cooking times, but once you get to know your own slow cooker, the possibilities will be endless, from midweek meals to impressive dinner party dishes, as well as desserts, cakes, and even breads.

TYPES AND SIZES OF SLOW COOKER

Available with a variety of features, slow cookers also come in a range of shapes and sizes, from 4.5-litre (5-quart) to 6.5-litre (7-quart) capacity. If you have a smaller or larger cooker than the recipe directs, you will need to decrease or increase the quantity of food, as well as the liquid content, too. Before using your cooker for the first time, read the manufacturer's instructions as each slow cooker will differ depending on its features. They will also outline appropriate safety measures, such as not leaving the appliance unattended at any time and making sure the cooker sits securely on a flat surface.

USING YOUR SLOW COOKER

As tempting as it is to check on your meal while it's cooking, lifting the lid constantly causes heat to escape and can set the cooking time back by up to half an hour each time.

The condensation that you can see on the lid of your slow cooker is the evaporation of moisture from the meat, sauce, and vegetables. As this liquid evaporates it hits the lid, gently drips down onto the food, and slowly bastes the meat as it cooks, ensuring perfectly tender meat and a rich sauce.

HEAT SETTINGS

A general rule of thumb is that high heat settings on a slow cooker will cook twice as fast as the lower setting. Generally, the longer meat takes to cook the more tender and flavoursome it will be.

BROWNING MEAT

For meat-based recipes, it is important to brown the meat first as it enhances the flavour and gives it a beautiful rich colour. Prep time for these recipes may be more like 20–25 minutes. Do this in a preheated, oiled, large frying pan, adding the meat in batches, and turning it so that it browns evenly. Make sure there is enough oil in the pan so that the meat caramelizes rather than scorches. Be sure to maintain the heat during browning; if the pan is not hot enough the meat will stew rather than brown. If your slow cooker has a sauté mode, use this to brown meat, in batches, just as you would in a frying pan.

LEFTOVER LIQUID

Any cooking liquid or sauce left over after cooking whole pieces of meat or poultry can be frozen separately and used as a base for another recipe such as a soup or a sauce.

5 BEST FOODS TO COOK IN THE SLOW COOKER

1. **MELT-IN-THE-MOUTH STEWS**
2. **BATCH COOKS FOR THE FREEZER**
3. **FLAVOURSOME CURRIES**
4. **BRAISED MEATS**
5. **GOOEY PUDDINGS**

FREEZING BATCH COOKS

Slow-cooked foods are luxurious and flavourful, and can be enjoyed equally when friends come over or as an easy weeknight dinner. They also freeze beautifully, giving you a wonderful comforting meal at the ready. Take a look at the Batch Cooking chapter for great recipes to make ahead and stock the freezer. When frozen properly, slow-cooked meals will keep for up to 3 months. Transfer the meat and vegetables to appropriate-sized freezer-friendly containers, then pour in enough of the liquid to cover. Leave a 2.5cm (1-inch) gap between the food and the lid to allow for expansion, then seal the container. Label and date the container, before placing in the freezer.

SLOW COOKER PUDS

No meal is complete without a little something sweet and the slow cooker delivers here, too. Puddings and even yeasted doughs can all be done in the slow cooker with great success. Serve with cream or ice cream for a low-fuss dessert.

SIMPLE SIDES

Try these alongside slow-cooked dishes:

Honey-glazed greens Cut a cavolo nero in half crossways and fry in extra virgin olive oil for 5 minutes until wilted. Add a handful of baby kale and 2 teaspoons honey, and toss for a minute until wilted. Top with crushed toasted pumpkin seeds.

Bistro side salad Combine 80ml (⅓ cup) white wine vinegar, 2 teaspoons Dijon mustard, and 2 teaspoons finely chopped thyme leaves in a small bowl. Gradually add 160ml (⅔ cup) olive oil, whisking constantly until thickened. Stir in 1 thinly sliced shallot and season to taste. Arrange 125g (4oz) rocket, 200g (7oz) cherry tomatoes, and 2 tablespoons mixed micro herbs onto a serving platter. Drizzle with the dressing.

Proscuitto crumb mash Fry 100g (3½oz) prosciutto slices in olive oil, for 5 minutes until crisp, then drain on kitchen paper. Sprinkle onto mashed potatoes along with thinly sliced spring onions.

Cheesy pull-apart rolls Mix 2 crushed garlic cloves, 2 tablespoons olive oil, and 1 tablespoon finely chopped parsley and season. Brush 12 mini dinner rolls with the oil mixture and arrange in a 23cm (9-inch) round cake pan. Sprinkle grated mozzarella on top and grill for 5 minutes.

EASY WEEKNIGHTS

The slow cooker is a great help for getting food on the table quickly on busy weeknights. Spend a little time getting the ingredients prepared and into the slow cooker in the morning, and you can enjoy perfectly cooked jacket potatoes, a hearty ragù, or slow-cooked meat that evening.

WHOLE SAUSAGE & ROSEMARY RAGÙ

1½ tbsp olive oil
1kg (2¼lb) thick pork and fennel sausages
1 onion, finely chopped
1 carrot, finely chopped
2 celery stalks, thinly sliced
1 tsp fennel seeds, or to taste
pinch of chilli flakes
4 cloves of garlic, crushed
125ml (½ cup) white wine
400g (14oz) can chopped tomatoes
250ml (1 cup) chicken stock
2 small sprigs of rosemary
2 tsp red wine vinegar
salt and freshly ground black pepper

TO SERVE:
your favourite pasta
grated Parmesan
basil leaves

1 Heat the oil in a large frying pan over medium–high heat. Cook the sausages, in batches, turning occasionally, for 6 minutes, or until browned all over. Transfer to a 5.5-litre (6-quart) slow cooker.

2 In the same frying pan, cook the onion, carrot, celery, fennel seeds, and chilli flakes, stirring occasionally, for 6 minutes, or until the vegetables are golden.

3 Add the garlic and cook, stirring, for 30 seconds, or until fragrant. Add the wine and bring to the boil, then reduce the heat and simmer for 5 minutes, or until reduced by half.

4 Season with salt and pepper, then transfer to the slow cooker. Add the canned tomatoes, stock, and rosemary, then stir to combine.

5 Cook, covered, on low, for 8 hours, or until the sausages are very tender. Remove the rosemary sprigs, stir through the vinegar, and season with salt and pepper to taste.

6 Serve the sausage ragù on pasta, topped with Parmesan and basil leaves.

**Prep + cook time
20 minutes + 8 hours
Serves 4**

CHIPOTLE BEAN TACOS

---

1 tbsp olive oil
1 red onion, chopped
6 cloves of garlic, bruised
1½ tsp cumin seeds
2½ tbsp chipotle in adobo sauce
3 x 400g (14oz) cans black beans, drained and rinsed
500ml (2 cups) vegetable stock
1 tbsp lime juice
500g (1lb 2oz) small corn tortillas
100g (3½oz) feta, crumbled
salt and freshly ground black pepper

PICKLED CABBAGE:
160g (2 cups) shredded red cabbage
60ml (¼ cup) lime juice
1 tsp caster sugar

TO SERVE:
coriander leaves
sliced spring onions
green hot sauce

1 Heat the oil in a large saucepan over medium–high heat. Cook the onion, garlic, and cumin for 5 minutes, or until the onion softens. Add the chipotle in sauce and cook, stirring, for 1 minute, or until fragrant.
2 Transfer to a 5-litre (5-quart) slow cooker. Add the black beans and stock, and stir to combine. Cook, covered, on low for 4 hours. Season to taste.
3 About 15 minutes before the end of the cooking time, make the pickled cabbage. Place the cabbage, lime juice, sugar, and 1 tablespoon water in a bowl and mix well. Let it stand for 15 minutes, stirring occasionally. Drain just before serving.
4 Coarsely mash the beans in the slow cooker, stir in the lime juice, and season.
5 Warm the corn tortillas following the packet instructions.
6 To serve, spoon the beans on the tortillas, then top with pickled cabbage and feta. Serve with coriander, spring onions, and hot sauce.

Prep + cook time
15 minutes + 4 hours
Serves 6

SPICY UPSIDE-DOWN PINEAPPLE CHICKEN

1 onion, roughly chopped
2 cloves of garlic, chopped
2½ tbsp grated fresh ginger
2 long green chillies, roughly chopped
1 lemongrass stalk, white part only, finely chopped
small handful of coriander, leaves and stems separated
2 tsp ground coriander
60ml (¼ cup) lime juice
2½ tbsp light soy sauce
2kg (4½lb) whole chicken, butterflied (see tip)
1 small pineapple, peeled, cored, and cut into 1cm (½-inch) rounds
300g (1½ cups) jasmine rice, rinsed
salt and freshly ground black pepper
olive oil cooking spray

1 Put the onion, garlic, ginger, chillies, lemongrass, coriander stems (reserve the leaves for garnishing), ground coriander, lime juice, and soy sauce in a food processor, and pulse until finely chopped.
2 Transfer the onion mixture to a large bowl, add the chicken, and turn to coat the chicken completely in the paste.
3 Place the pineapple slices, slightly overlapping, over the base of a 6-litre (6½-quart) slow cooker. Top with the chicken, breast-side down, and the onion mixture. Cook, covered, on low for 4 hours, or until the chicken is tender.
4 Line a baking tray with foil. Carefully transfer the chicken, skin-side up, to the tray, followed by the pineapple rings.
5 Add the rice to the slow cooker and stir.
6 Cook the rice, covered, on low for 35 minutes.
7 Season the rice, turn off the slow cooker, and let it stand for 10 minutes.
8 Meanwhile, preheat the grill to high. Lightly spray the chicken and pineapple with olive oil. Place under the grill for 10 minutes, or until the chicken is golden brown.
9 Serve the chicken and pineapple with the rice and coriander leaves.

TIP To butterfly a chicken, place the chicken breast-side down on a chopping board. Cut down both sides of the backbone using a pair of kitchen scissors. Discard the backbone. Turn the chicken over. Press firmly with the heel of your hand to flatten.

Prep + cook time
15 minutes + 4 hours
35 minutes, plus standing
Serves 4

MIXED MUSHROOM & LENTIL RAGÙ

400g (14oz) king oyster mushrooms
400g (14oz) portobello mushrooms
400g (14oz) chestnut mushrooms
60ml (¼ cup) olive oil
1 onion, roughly chopped
1 large carrot, roughly chopped
2 celery stalks, roughly chopped
180ml (¾ cup) red wine
20g (¾oz) dried porcini mushrooms
1½ tbsp harissa paste
500ml (2 cups) vegetable stock
2 fresh bay leaves
400g (14oz) can cherry tomatoes
200g (1 cup) dried black lentils, rinsed
salt and freshly ground black pepper

TO SERVE:
creamy polenta

1 Place half of each variety of mushroom in a food processor and pulse until coarsely chopped. Transfer to a bowl.
2 Heat half the oil in a large, deep frying pan over medium–high heat. Add the chopped mushrooms and cook, stirring occasionally, for 5 minutes, or until softened and browned. Transfer to a 6-litre (6½-quart) slow cooker.
3 Heat the remaining oil in the same frying pan over high heat. Add the remaining whole mushrooms and cook for 4 minutes, stirring, until browned. Transfer to the slow cooker.
4 Add the onion, carrot, and celery to the same frying pan and cook, stirring, for 5 minutes, or until softened.
5 Add the red wine and porcini, and cook for 3 minutes, or until most of the liquid has evaporated.
6 Stir in the harissa paste and cook, stirring, for 30 seconds, or until fragrant. Add the stock, bay leaves, canned tomatoes, and lentils, and season with salt and pepper. Transfer the mixture to the slow cooker and stir to combine. Cook, covered, on low for 4 hours.
7 Serve the ragù with creamy polenta.

**Prep + cook time
20 minutes + 4 hours
Serves 4**

CHICKEN, LEEK & CIDER CASSEROLE

70g (½ cup) plain flour
2kg (4½lb) skinless chicken thighs
60g (½ stick) unsalted butter, chopped
8 cloves of garlic, bruised
2 leeks, halved and cut into 5cm (2-inch) pieces
2 large Pink Lady apples, cut into wedges
6 sprigs of thyme, plus extra to serve
70g (¼ cup) wholegrain mustard
330ml (1⅓ cups) cider
250ml (1 cup) chicken stock
salt and freshly ground black pepper

CHEESE TOASTS:
1 small sourdough baguette, thickly sliced
1 clove of garlic, halved
200g (7oz) Cheddar, thinly sliced
35g (¼ cup) roasted hazelnuts, roughly chopped

TO SERVE:
crème fraîche

1 Place the flour in a large bowl, season with salt and pepper, and add the chicken. Toss to coat well.

2 Heat half the butter in a large frying pan over medium–high heat. Cook the chicken, in batches, for 6 minutes, or until browned all over. Transfer to a 5-litre (5-quart) slow cooker.

3 Add the garlic, leeks, apples, thyme, mustard, cider, and stock and stir to combine. Cook, covered, on low for 4 hours, or until the chicken is tender. Season to taste.

4 About 10 minutes before the end of the cooking time, preheat the grill to high for the cheese toasts. Place the bread in a single layer on a foil-lined oven tray. Grill for 2 minutes on each side, or until lightly golden. Rub the toasts with the garlic, top with cheese and hazelnuts, and grill for 3 minutes until melted.

5 Divide the casserole among bowls, top with extra thyme, and serve with the cheese toasts and some crème fraîche on the side.

**Prep + cook time
15 minutes + 4 hours
Serves 6**

HERBY LEMON LAMB SHOULDER

60ml (¼ cup) olive oil
1.8kg (4lb) lamb shoulder, bone in
4 cloves of garlic, crushed
2½ tbsp finely grated lemon zest
4 sprigs of rosemary, leaves picked and finely chopped
5 tbsp oregano leaves, finely chopped
2½ tbsp thyme leaves
500ml (2 cups) chicken stock
500g (1lb 2oz) baby potatoes
8 pickling onions, peeled
salt and freshly ground black pepper

HERB DRESSING:
5 tbsp flat-leaf parsley leaves
5 tbsp mint leaves
5 tbsp tarragon leaves
80ml (⅓ cup) olive oil

1 Heat a large non-stick frying pan over high heat. Add 1 tablespoon olive oil and the lamb and cook for 12 minutes, or until browned all over. Transfer to a 6.5-litre (7-quart) slow cooker.
2 Combine the garlic, lemon zest, herbs, and remaining olive oil in a small bowl.
3 Spread the herb mixture over the lamb. Add the stock to the slow cooker, stir to combine, and season. Cook, covered, on low for 5 hours.
4 Add the potatoes and onions to the slow cooker and stir to combine. Cook, covered, for a further 4 hours, or until the lamb is very tender.
5 Carefully remove the lamb and vegetables from the slow cooker; cover to keep warm.
6 Strain the cooking liquid into a saucepan and bring to the boil over high heat, then reduce the heat and simmer for 10 minutes, or until the liquid has reduced by two-thirds; you should have approximately 250ml (1 cup) left.
7 Make the herb dressing by putting the ingredients in a blender and pulsing until smooth. Season to taste.
8 Serve the lamb, potatoes, and onions with the pan juices and herby dressing.

Prep + cook time
15 minutes + 9 hours
10 minutes
Serves 4–6

CRISPY CHILLI PEANUT CHICKEN

1½ tbsp vegetable oil
8 chicken drumsticks, about 1kg (2¼lb)
1 red pepper, thickly sliced
4 spring onions, cut into 3cm (1¼-inch) lengths, plus extra, shredded, to serve
120g (⅓ cup) honey
80ml (⅓ cup) rice wine vinegar
60ml (¼ cup) light soy sauce
2 tbsp crispy peanut chilli oil (see tip)
5cm (2-inch) piece fresh ginger, finely grated
1½ tbsp cornflour
salt and freshly ground black pepper

TO SERVE:
steamed rice
Chinese broccoli

1 Heat the oil in a large frying pan over high heat. Cook the chicken, in batches, for 6 minutes, or until browned all over. Transfer the chicken to a 4.5-litre (5-quart) slow cooker.
2 Add the red pepper, spring onions, honey, vinegar, soy sauce, chilli oil, and ginger to the slow cooker.
3 Combine the cornflour with 125ml (½ cup) water in a small bowl until smooth. Add to the slow cooker and stir to combine.
4 Cook, covered, on low for 4 hours, or until the chicken is very tender. Season to taste.
5 Serve the chicken with rice and Chinese broccoli, topped with extra shredded spring onions.

TIP Crispy peanut chilli oil is available from most major supermarkets in the Asian food section.

Prep + cook time
15 minutes + 4 hours
Serves 4

BUTTERNUT SQUASH & GOAT'S CHEESE BARLEY RISOTTO

30g (2 tbsp) butter
1 leek, thinly sliced
1½ tbsp chopped thyme, plus extra to serve
2 cloves of garlic, crushed
125ml (½ cup) dry white wine
½ butternut squash, peeled and cut into 2cm (¾-inch) pieces
250g (1½ cups) pearl barley, rinsed
50g (⅓ cup) sun-dried tomatoes
1.25 litres (5 cups) vegetable stock
60g (¾ cup) finely grated Parmesan
120g (4oz) goat's cheese, crumbled
salt and freshly ground black pepper

1 Melt the butter in a large frying pan over medium–high heat, add the leek, thyme, and garlic, and cook, stirring, for 5 minutes until the leek softens.

2 Add the wine and bring to the boil, then reduce the heat to low and simmer for 5 minutes, or until reduced by half.

3 Transfer to a 4.5-litre (5-quart) slow cooker. Add the butternut squash, barley, sun-dried tomatoes, and stock, and stir to combine. Cook, covered, on low for 6 hours, or until the barley is tender.

4 Stir in the Parmesan and season to taste.

5 Spoon the risotto into bowls, top with the goat's cheese and extra thyme, and serve immediately.

SERVE IT This risotto works well with a peppery rocket salad on the side.

Prep + cook time
15 minutes + 6 hours
Serves 6

LAMB CHOPS & BROWN RICE PILAF

60ml (¼ cup) olive oil
1 small onion, finely chopped
300g (1½ cups) brown rice
500ml (2 cups) chicken stock
1½ tsp ground cumin
1½ tsp ground coriander
1½ tsp ground cinnamon
8 lamb neck chops, about 800g (1¾lb)
handful of flat-leaf parsley, chopped, plus extra leaves to serve
100g (3½oz) feta, crumbled
40g (¼ cup) currants

PICKLED ONION:
1 large red onion, thinly sliced
60ml (¼ cup) red wine vinegar
1½ tbsp caster sugar
2 tsp sea salt flakes

1 Heat half the oil in a large frying pan over medium–high heat. Add the onion and cook, stirring, for 3 minutes, or until softened. Add the rice and stir to combine. Transfer to a 5-litre (5-quart) slow cooker.
2 Add the stock to the same frying pan, bring to the boil, then reduce the heat and simmer for 2 minutes. Pour the hot stock over the rice in the slow cooker. Cook, covered, on low for 1 hour.
3 Combine the spices in a large bowl, add the lamb, and coat in the spices.
4 Heat the remaining oil in the same frying pan over medium–high heat. Cook the lamb, in batches, for 2 minutes on each side, or until browned all over.
5 Place the lamb on the rice in the slow cooker. Cook, covered, for 3 hours, or until the lamb is tender.
6 About 30 minutes before the end of the cooking time, combine the pickled onion ingredients in a small bowl. Leave to stand for 30 minutes, stirring occasionally. Drain just before serving
7 Carefully remove the lamb from the slow cooker. When cool enough to handle, remove the meat from the bones and shred coarsely using two forks. Return the shredded lamb to the slow cooker with the chopped parsley, and stir to combine with the rice.
8 Top with the feta, currants, pickled onion, and extra parsley leaves and serve.

**Prep + cook time
20 minutes + 4 hours
Serves 4–6**

BEEF SHORT RIB BAO

2½ tbsp vegetable oil
12 beef short ribs, about 2.4kg (5¼lb)
1 large onion, thickly sliced
125ml (½ cup) soy sauce
2½ tbsp rice wine vinegar
2½ tbsp gochujang (Korean chilli paste)
8 cloves of garlic, bruised
5cm (2-inch) piece fresh ginger, thinly sliced
50g (¼ cup) brown sugar
1½ tbsp sesame oil
1 tsp freshly ground black pepper
1½ tbsp cornflour
14 bao buns

PICKLED CUCUMBER:
250g (9oz) baby cucumbers, quartered lengthways
125ml (½ cup) rice wine vinegar
2½ tbsp caster sugar

TO SERVE:
Japanese mayonnaise
coriander leaves
chilli slices

1 Heat half the vegetable oil in a large frying pan over high heat. Add half the beef and half the onion, and cook, stirring, for 6 minutes, or until browned all over. Transfer to a 5.5-litre (6-quart) slow cooker. Repeat with the remaining vegetable oil, beef, and onion.

2 Combine the soy, vinegar, gochujang, garlic, ginger, sugar, sesame oil, and pepper in a large jug. Pour over the beef in the slow cooker, then cover the slow cooker with a clean tea towel. Place the lid on top, then fold the towel up over the lid. Cook, covered, on low for 7 hours, or until the beef is tender.

4 Carefully remove the beef from the slow cooker and shred the meat coarsely using two forks; discard the bones. Cover to keep warm.

5 Strain the cooking liquid into a saucepan, discarding any solids.

6 Combine the cornflour with 2 tablespoons water in a small bowl until smooth. Add to the strained cooking liquid and cook, stirring continuously, over medium heat for 1 minute, or until thick and glossy. Add the shredded beef and stir to coat in the sauce. Cover to keep warm.

7 Meanwhile, place the pickled cucumber ingredients in a bowl with 125ml (½ cup) water and mix well. Let it stand for 10 minutes, stirring occasionally. Drain just before serving.

8 Heat the bao buns according to the packet instructions.

9 Fill the buns with the beef mixture, then top with pickled cucumbers, Japanese mayonnaise, coriander, and chilli.

**Prep + cook time
20 minutes + 7 hours 5 minutes, plus standing
Makes 14**

BRAISED PORK WITH PINEAPPLE & SWEET CHILLI

1½ tbsp vegetable oil
1kg (2¼lb) piece pork shoulder, cut into 6cm (2½-inch) pieces
1 red onion, thinly sliced
2 large cloves of garlic, crushed
2 tbsp finely grated fresh ginger
½ pineapple, peeled, cored, and roughly chopped
80ml (⅓ cup) sweet chilli sauce
2½ tbsp fish sauce
1½ tbsp reduced-salt soy sauce
2 tsp white wine vinegar
4 makrut lime leaves, plus extra, shredded, to serve
2 star anise
200g (7oz) green beans, trimmed and halved
1½ tbsp lime juice
salt and freshly ground black pepper

TO SERVE:
Thai basil leaves
roasted cashews
rice noodles
lime wedges

1 Heat the oil in a large frying pan over medium–high heat. Cook the pork, turning occasionally, for 4 minutes, or until browned all over. Transfer the pork to a 5.5-litre (6-quart) slow cooker.
2 Add 125ml (½ cup) water to the same frying pan, bring to the boil, then reduce the heat and simmer for 5 minutes, or until reduced by half.
3 Transfer the reduced liquid to the slow cooker, then add the onion, garlic, ginger, pineapple, sauces, vinegar, lime leaves, and star anise. Cook, covered, on low for 7 hours 30 minutes.
4 Add the beans and cook, covered, on low for 30 minutes, or until the beans are tender.
5 Remove the lime leaves. Stir in the lime juice and season to taste.
6 Top the pork with Thai basil, extra lime leaves, and roasted cashews. Serve with rice noodles and lime wedges.

**Prep + cook time
15 minutes + 8 hours
Serves 4–6**

BACON, CHEESE & SOUR CREAM JACKET POTATOES

---

6 large baking potatoes
1½ tbsp extra virgin olive oil
1 tsp sea salt flakes
200g (7oz) rindless bacon rashers
30g (2 tbsp) butter, cut into 6 pieces
90g (1 cup) grated Cheddar
240g (1 cup) sour cream
2½ tbsp chopped chives

1 Place the potatoes, oil, and salt flakes in a large bowl and turn to coat well all over.
2 Wrap each potato, separately, in foil. Place the potatoes, seam-side up, in a 4.5-litre (5-quart) slow cooker. Cook, covered, on low for 8 hours.
3 Heat a large non-stick frying pan over high heat and cook the bacon for 3 minutes on each side, or until crisp. Drain on kitchen paper and coarsely chop.
4 Carefully remove the potatoes from the slow cooker with tongs. When cool enough to handle, remove the foil.
5 Cut a 2.5cm- (1-inch-) deep slit lengthways down the centre of each potato. Gently squeeze the base of each potato to open it up. Transfer to a foil-lined oven tray.
6 Preheat the grill to high. Top each potato with a piece of butter, sprinkle evenly with cheese, and season with salt and pepper. Place under the grill for 4 minutes, or until the cheese has melted.
7 Serve the potatoes topped with the sour cream, bacon, and chives.

Prep + cook time
10 minutes + 8 hours
10 minutes
Makes 6

SWEET POTATO, TURMERIC & LENTIL SOUP

1½ tbsp olive oil
1 large onion, diced
2 cloves of garlic, crushed
1½ tbsp finely grated fresh ginger
1½ tbsp finely grated fresh turmeric (see tip)
1kg (2¼lb) orange-fleshed sweet potatoes, roughly chopped
300g (10½oz) carrots, roughly chopped
200g (1 cup) red lentils
1.5 litres (6 cups) vegetable stock
400ml (14oz) can coconut milk
salt and freshly ground black pepper

TO SERVE:
coriander sprigs
crusty bread

1 Heat the oil in a large frying pan over medium–high heat, add the onion, garlic, ginger, and turmeric, and cook, stirring, for 5 minutes, or until the onion softens. Transfer to a 4.5-litre (5-quart) slow cooker.

2 Add the sweet potatoes, carrots, lentils, stock, and coconut milk to the slow cooker, season, and stir to combine. Cook, covered, on low for 5 hours.

3 Ladle the soup into bowls, top with coriander, and serve with crusty bread on the side.

TIP If fresh turmeric is hard to find, you can use the same amount of ground turmeric instead.

**Prep + cook time
15 minutes + 5 hours
Serves 4–6**

HERB & WALNUT FRITTATA

60g (2 cups) baby spinach leaves
2 good handfuls of flat-leaf parsley leaves
handful of mint leaves
handful of dill
12 eggs, beaten lightly
70g (⅓ cup) Greek yogurt, plus extra to serve
100g (1 cup) roasted walnuts, roughly chopped
65g (½ cup) dried cranberries, roughly chopped
2 tsp sumac
salt and freshly ground black pepper

TO SERVE (OPTIONAL):
flaked smoked trout
lemon wedges
extra virgin olive oil

1 Remove the pot from a 4.5-litre (5-quart) slow cooker. Line the base of the pot with two layers of baking paper, then return to the slow cooker.
2 Place the spinach and half of each herb in a food processor, and pulse until coarsely chopped. Add the egg and yogurt, and pulse until just combined. Stir in the walnuts, cranberries, and sumac, and season with salt and pepper.
3 Pour the mixture into the slow cooker, cover with a clean tea towel, place the lid on top, then fold the towel up over the lid. Cook on low for 4 hours, or until set. Turn the slow cooker off and let it stand for 10 minutes.
4 Meanwhile, place the remaining herbs in a bowl and toss gently to combine.
5 Serve the frittata cut into wedges with, if liked, smoked trout, extra yogurt, herb salad, and lemon wedges. If you like, drizzle with a little extra virgin olive oil.

Prep + cook time
15 minutes + 4 hours,
plus standing
Serves 4–6

SWEET & SALTY CHICKEN WINGS

1½ tbsp vegetable oil
2kg (4½lb) chicken wings, separated at the joint and wing tips discarded
80ml (⅓ cup) barbecue sauce
80ml (⅓ cup) sweet chilli sauce
80ml (⅓ cup) soy sauce
75g (⅓ cup) brown sugar
4 cloves of garlic, crushed
200g (7oz) shop-bought coleslaw
75g (¼ cup) mayonnaise
1½ tbsp white wine vinegar
2 spring onions, thinly sliced
salt and freshly ground black pepper

TO SERVE:
French fries

1 Heat the oil in a large frying pan over medium–high heat. Cook the chicken, in batches, for 10 minutes, turning regularly, or until browned all over. Transfer to a 6-litre (6½-quart) slow cooker.
2 Combine the sauces, sugar, and garlic in a jug and season. Pour over the chicken in the slow cooker and mix well to coat. Arrange the wings in an even layer and cook, covered, on low for 3 hours 30 minutes.
3 Transfer the wings to a large oven tray. Strain the cooking liquid from the slow cooker into a medium saucepan over high heat. Bring to the boil, then reduce the heat and simmer for 10 minutes, or until the sauce has thickened. Keep warm.
4 Meanwhile, preheat the grill. Place the wings under the grill and cook for 5 minutes, turning halfway, until browned and the skins are crisp.
5 Place the coleslaw, mayonnaise, and vinegar in a large bowl and season. Mix well to combine.
6 Drizzle the sauce over the wings, top with spring onions, and serve with the coleslaw and French fries.

Prep + cook time
20 minutes + 3 hours
40 minutes
Serves 4

BEEF RAGÙ WITH TORN PASTA SHEETS

2 carrots, chopped
2 celery stalks, chopped
1 onion, chopped
270g (9½oz) jar sun-dried tomato strips in oil, drained
80ml (⅓ cup) extra virgin olive oil
800g (1¾lb) chuck steak, cut into 5cm (2-inch) pieces
500g (1lb 2oz) minced beef
250ml (1 cup) red wine
250ml (1 cup) chicken stock
2 x 400g (14oz) cans chopped tomatoes
2 bay leaves
375g (13oz) fresh lasagne sheets, torn
250g (9oz) buffalo mozzarella, torn
small bunch of sage leaves

1 Put the carrots, celery, onion, and sun-dried tomatoes in a food processor and blitz until finely chopped.
2 Heat 2 tablespoons of the oil in a large heavy-based frying pan over high heat. Cook the chuck steak, in batches, turning occasionally, for 6 minutes, or until browned all over. Transfer to a 6-litre (6½-quart) slow cooker.
3 Add the finely chopped vegetables to the same frying pan over medium heat, and cook, stirring occasionally, for 4 minutes, or until just softened. Transfer to the slow cooker, then add the mince, wine, stock, tomatoes, and bay leaves. Season, then cook, covered, on low for 6 hours.
4 Carefully remove the chuck steak from the slow cooker and shred the meat coarsely using two forks. Return the meat to the slow cooker.
5 Add the torn lasagne sheets and stir to combine. Top with the mozzarella. Cook, covered, on low for a further 1 hour 30 minutes.
6 Heat the remaining oil in a small frying pan over medium heat. Cook the sage leaves, in batches, for 30 seconds, or until crisp. Drain on kitchen paper.
7 Serve the ragù in bowls topped with the crisp sage leaves.

Prep + cook time
20 minutes + 7 hours
30 minutes
Serves 4–6

DEEP-PAN PEPPERONI PIZZA

olive oil cooking spray
2 x 250g (9oz) balls of store-bought fresh pizza dough (see tip)
85g (⅓ cup) garlic, onion, and herb pizza sauce
65g (⅔ cup) grated mozzarella
80g (2½oz) sliced pepperoni
1 small green pepper, thinly sliced
½ small red onion, thinly sliced
100g (3½oz) sliced button mushrooms
handful of small basil leaves

1 Remove the pot from a 6-litre (6½-quart) oval slow cooker. Line the base and long sides with two layers of baking paper, allowing the papers to come halfway up the sides. Spray well with oil.
2 Remove the pizza dough from their packets and knead together lightly to form one ball. Place the dough in the lined pot, return it to the slow cooker, and cover with the lid. Set the slow cooker to low and leave to prove for 30 minutes.
3 Adjust the slow cooker setting to high. Push the dough down lightly, pressing it out to cover the base and create a thick rim. Spread the pizza sauce over the dough, top with half the cheese, the pepperoni, pepper, onion, and mushrooms. Cook, covered, for 2 hours.
4 Preheat the grill to medium.
5 Using the lining paper, lift the pizza out of the slow cooker onto an oven tray. Sprinkle with the remaining cheese.
6 Place under the grill for 10 minutes, or until the cheese and crust are browned. Top with the basil leaves and serve.

TIP Ready-made pizza dough is available in most supermarkets; you'll find it in the refrigerated section.

Prep + cook time
10 minutes + 2 hours
40 minutes
Serves 4

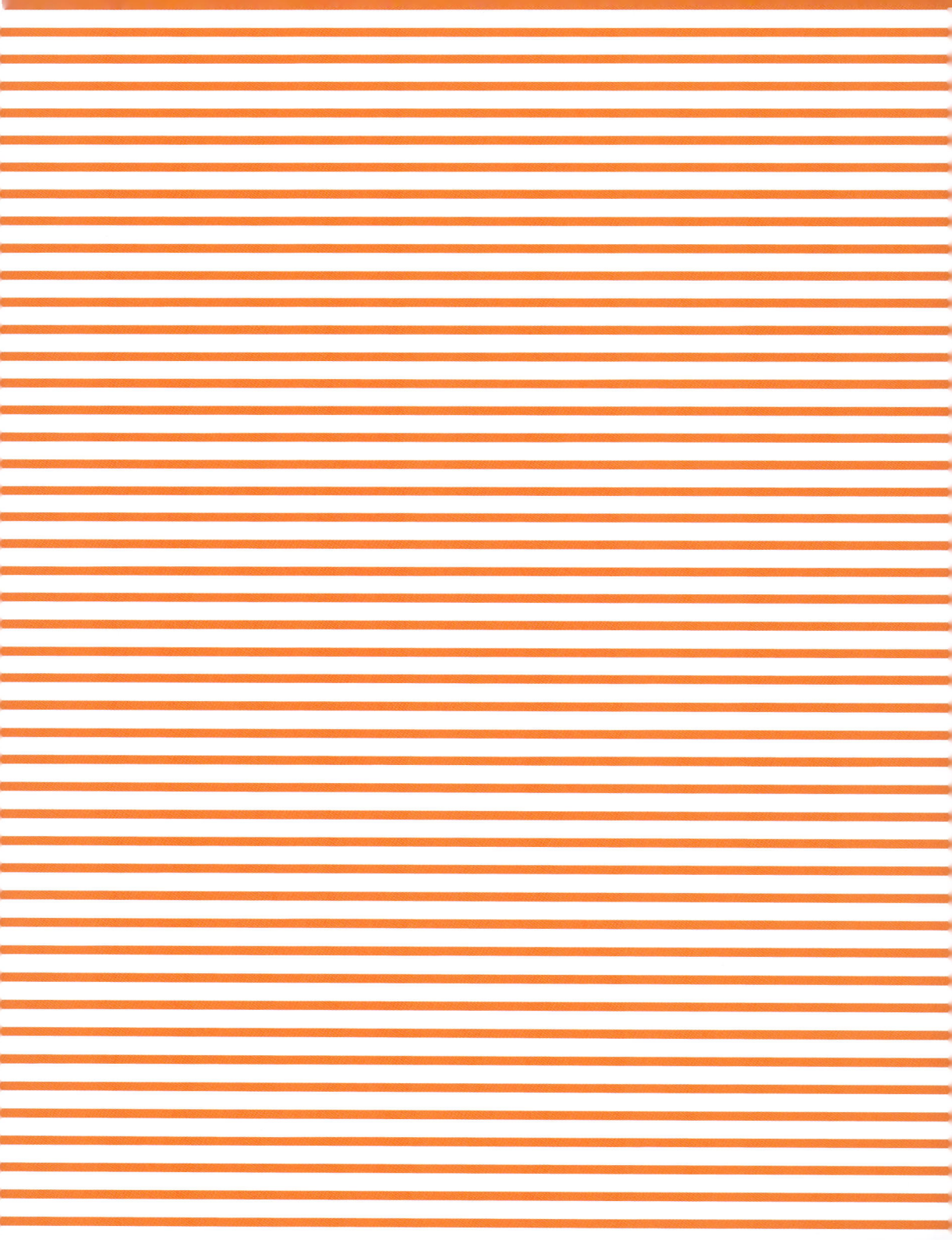

CURRIES, SOUPS & STEWS

When you think of the slow cooker, these are the recipes that come to mind: melt-in-the-mouth stews, slow-cooked to perfection; warming curries full of tender meat and veggies; and nourishing, flavour-packed soups.

THAI COCONUT & CHICKEN SOUP

195g (7oz) jar Thai red curry paste
2 lemongrass stalks, bruised
4cm (1½-inch) piece fresh ginger, finely grated
6 makrut lime leaves, lightly crushed with your hands
800g (1¾lb) chicken thigh fillets, cut into 3cm (1¼-inch) pieces
250g (9oz) small button mushrooms, larger ones halved
1 litre (4 cups) chicken stock
400ml (14oz) can coconut milk
1½ tbsp fish sauce
1½ tbsp grated palm sugar

TO SERVE:
Thai basil
lime wedges

1 Preheat a 6-litre (6½-quart) slow cooker on high.
2 Place the curry paste, lemongrass, ginger, and lime leaves in the heated slow cooker. Cook, stirring occasionally, for 5 minutes, or until fragrant.
3 Add the chicken and mushrooms to the slow cooker and stir until well coated in the mixture. Add the stock, coconut milk, and fish sauce, then stir in the palm sugar.
4 Turn the slow cooker to low and cook, covered, for 5 hours.
5 Serve the soup topped with Thai basil and with lime wedges for squeezing.

Prep + cook time
15 minutes +
5 hours 5 minutes
Serves 4

SPICED ALMOND CHICKEN RICE

80g (⅓ cup) ghee, or 80g (¾ stick) butter
1 large red onion, thinly sliced
300g (1½ cups) extra-long grain premium basmati rice (see tip)
1½ tbsp garam masala
2 tsp ground coriander
1 tsp ground turmeric
½ tsp ground chilli powder
1 cinnamon stick
6 green cardamom pods, bruised
70g (scant 1 cup) flaked almonds
6 small chicken thigh fillets, about 600g (1lb 5oz), quartered
200g (scant 1 cup) Greek yogurt, plus extra to serve
2 tsp grated fresh ginger
1 clove of garlic, crushed
180ml (¾ cup) chicken stock
50g (⅓ cup) raisins
salt and freshly ground black pepper

TO SERVE:
tomato slices
coriander leaves

1 Melt the ghee in a large frying pan with a lid over medium–high heat. Add the onion and cook, covered, for 6 minutes, or until soft and starting to brown on the edges.
2 Meanwhile, place the rice in a sieve and rinse under hot running water until the water runs clear. Drain.
3 Add the ground spices, whole spices, and almonds to the onion in the frying pan, and cook, uncovered, for 2 minutes until toasted.
4 Spoon half the onion mixture into a 4.5-litre (5-quart) slow cooker. Add the chicken, yogurt, ginger, and garlic, then season and mix well.
5 Spread the drained rice over the chicken mixture, then pour over the stock. Top with the remaining onion mixture and any ghee in the pan. Scatter the raisins on top.
6 Cook, covered, on low for 4 hours.
7 Serve with extra yogurt, tomato slices, and coriander leaves.

TIP It is important to use good-quality basmati rice for this recipe. An extra-long grain variety gives a fluffier result.

Prep + cook time
15 minutes +
4 hours 15 minutes
Serves 4

PENANG BEEF CURRY

2½ tbsp vegetable oil
3 beef cheeks, about 900g (2lb), cut into 6cm (2½-inch) pieces
400ml (14oz) can coconut milk
2½ tbsp fish sauce, or to taste
1½ tbsp lime juice, or to taste
1½ tbsp coconut sugar, or to taste

PENANG CURRY PASTE:
bunch of coriander
1 shallot, chopped
3 makrut lime leaves
2 cloves of garlic
2 long red chillies, roughly chopped
1 lemongrass stalk, white part only, roughly chopped
20g (¾oz) fresh galangal or ginger, roughly chopped
75g (generous ½ cup) salted peanuts, plus extra to serve
2 tsp ground cumin
1 tsp chilli powder
125ml (½ cup) vegetable oil

TO SERVE:
steamed Tenderstem broccoli
mangetout
steamed jasmine rice

1 First, make the Penang curry paste. Cut the stems from the coriander and set the leaves aside to serve. Place the stems in a blender with the remaining paste ingredients, and blend into a smooth paste. Set aside.
2 Heat the oil in a large frying pan over high heat. Cook the beef, turning occasionally, for 8 minutes, or until browned. Remove from the pan.
3 Reduce the heat under the frying pan to medium, add the curry paste, and cook, stirring, for 2 minutes until fragrant. Stir in the coconut milk.
4 Transfer the mixture to a 5.5-litre (6-quart) slow cooker, then add the beef. Cook, covered, on low for 6 hours.
5 Stir in the fish sauce, lime juice, and coconut sugar, and adjust to taste.
6 Top the curry with the reserved coriander leaves and extra peanuts, and serve with Tenderstem broccoli, mangetout, and jasmine rice.

Prep + cook time
15 minutes +
6 hours 15 minutes
Serves 4

BUTTERNUT SQUASH & TOMATO CURRY

1½ tbsp extra virgin olive oil
2 red onions, quartered
4 large cloves of garlic, bruised
1 tsp chilli flakes
1 cinnamon stick
6 star anise
750g (1lb 10oz) vine-ripened tomatoes, roughly chopped
2½ tbsp tomato purée
500ml (2 cups) vegetable stock
1.2kg (2½lb) whole butternut squash, halved and seeds removed
70g (2 cups) torn kale leaves
salt and freshly ground black pepper

TO SERVE:
steamed basmati rice

1 Heat the oil in a large, deep frying pan, add the onion, and cook, stirring, for 3 minutes, or until softened. Add the garlic and chilli flakes, and cook, stirring, for a further 30 seconds, or until fragrant. Add the spices, tomatoes, tomato purée, and stock, and season.

2 Transfer the mixture to a 6-litre (6½-quart) slow cooker. Place the butternut squash halves on top, cut-side up. Cook, covered, on low for 4 hours, or until the squash is tender.

3 Place the kale leaves on the butternut squash halves. Cook, covered, for a further 5 minutes, or until wilted.

4 Serve the curry with basmati rice.

**Prep + cook time
15 minutes +
4 hours 15 minutes
Serves 4**

AUBERGINE DAL WITH RAINBOW CHARD

60ml (¼ cup) extra virgin olive oil
2 aubergines, cut into 7cm (2¾-inch) pieces
8 shallots
1 tsp brown mustard seeds
2 tsp ground cumin
2 tsp ground coriander
½ tsp ground turmeric
1½ tbsp grated fresh ginger
150g (¾ cup) dried red lentils
2 long red chillies, halved lengthways
2 sprigs of curry leaves
400ml (14oz) can coconut milk
500ml (2 cups) vegetable stock
bunch of rainbow chard, about 750g (1lb 10oz), stalks removed and leaves torn (see tip)
75g (½ cup) roasted, unsalted cashews, roughly chopped
salt and freshly ground black pepper

TO SERVE:
steamed basmati rice
poppadoms

1 Heat the oil in a large, deep frying pan. Cook the aubergines, in two batches, turning occasionally, for 5 minutes, or until golden. Remove from the pan.
2 Cook the shallots in the same frying pan for 3 minutes, or until golden. Add the mustard seeds and cook, stirring, for 30 seconds, or until they begin to pop. Add the spices and ginger, and cook for 30 seconds, or until fragrant. Add the lentils, chillies, curry leaves, coconut milk, and stock. Stir to combine and season.
3 Transfer the lentil mixture to a 6-litre (6½-quart) slow cooker and top with the aubergines. Cook, covered, on low for 4 hours.
4 Stir in the chard leaves until wilted. Top the dal with the cashews, and serve with basmati rice and poppadoms.

TIP If you can't find rainbow chard you can use regular chard instead.

**Prep + cook time
15 minutes + 4 hours
Serves 4**

CHICKEN & COCONUT LAKSA

1½ tbsp peanut oil
8 chicken drumsticks, about 1kg (2¼lb)
400ml (14oz) can coconut milk
1.5 litres (6 cups) chicken stock
6 makrut lime leaves
1½ tbsp brown sugar
1½ tbsp fish sauce
1½ tbsp lime juice
200g (7oz) vermicelli rice noodles
500g (1lb 2oz) choy sum, chopped

LAKSA PASTE:
3 small dried red chillies
4cm (1½-inch) piece fresh ginger
4cm (1½-inch) piece fresh turmeric
4 shallots
2 long red chillies
1 lemongrass stalk, white part only
35g (¼ cup) macadamia halves
3 cloves of garlic
2 tsp roasted shrimp paste (belacan)
2 tsp ground coriander

TO SERVE:
tofu puffs
bean sprouts
coriander leaves
lime wedges

1 Heat the oil in a large frying pan over medium–high heat and cook the chicken, turning, for 5 minutes, or until browned all over. Transfer to a 4.5-litre (5-quart) slow cooker and keep the frying pan to one side.

2 To make the laksa paste, place the dried chillies in a heatproof bowl and cover with boiling water; let them soak for 5 minutes, then drain. Roughly chop the ginger and turmeric along with the shallots, fresh chillies, and lemongrass. Add to a food processor with the soaked chillies, macadamia, garlic, shrimp paste, and ground coriander. Process to a smooth paste.

3 Cook the laksa paste in the reserved frying pan over medium heat, stirring, until fragrant and roasted. Stir in the coconut milk.

4 Pour the laksa mixture over the chicken in the slow cooker.

5 Add the stock and lime leaves. Cook, covered, on low for 6 hours.

6 Season with the sugar, fish sauce, and lime juice, to taste. Remove the chicken, let cool slightly, then shred the meat coarsely and discard the bones.

7 Place the noodles in a large heatproof bowl with enough boiling water to cover. Place the choy sum on the noodles. Cover and leave for 5 minutes, or until the noodles soften. Drain.

8 Divide the noodles, choy sum, and chicken among bowls. Strain the laksa soup into a jug, then divide among the bowls. Serve the laksa topped with tofu puffs, bean sprouts, and coriander leaves, and with lime wedges on the side.

Prep + cook time
15 minutes + 6 hours
5 minutes
Serves 4

CABBAGE WITH CORIANDER CHUTNEY

60g (¼ cup) ghee
1 green cabbage, cut into 6 wedges (see tip)
5 cloves of garlic, bruised
1 green bird's eye chilli, thinly sliced
1 tsp cumin seeds
250ml (1 cup) vegetable stock
3 shallots, thinly sliced
1½ tsp brown mustard seeds
3 sprigs of curry leaves
75g (½ cup) roasted cashews

CORIANDER CHUTNEY:
100g (3½oz) coriander (stems and leaves), roughly chopped
1 clove of garlic
1 green bird's eye chilli, chopped
1 tsp cumin seeds
1½ tbsp lemon juice

TO SERVE:
naan bread

1 Heat 1 tablespoon of the ghee in a large frying pan over high heat. Cook the cabbage, cut-side down, for 5 minutes on each side, or until charred. Add the garlic, chilli, and cumin and cook for 2 minutes, or until fragrant. Stir in the stock.

2 Transfer the cabbage wedges, cut-side up, to a 6-litre (6½-quart) slow cooker. Pour over the stock mixture. Cook, covered, on low for 4 hours. Keep the frying pan to one side.

3 Meanwhile, make the coriander chutney. Put all the ingredients and 60ml (¼ cup) water in a blender and blend until smooth. Season to taste.

4 When the cabbage has 15 minutes left in the slow cooker, heat the remaining ghee in the reserved frying pan over medium–high heat. Cook the shallots, stirring occasionally, for 10 minutes, or until soft and golden.

5 Increase the heat to high. Add the mustard seeds and curry leaves and cook, stirring, for 2 minutes, or until the curry leaves are crisp. Stir in the cashews.

6 Serve the cabbage and sauce on a serving platter, topped with the cashew mixture. Serve with the coriander chutney and naan bread.

TIP When it is in season, use a sweetheart cabbage, which can be distinguished by its conical head and sweet taste.

Prep + cook time
15 minutes + 4 hours
Serves 4

GREEN CURRY BEEF RIBS

1½ tbsp olive oil
6 beef ribs, about 3kg (6½lb), halved (see tip)
3 shallots, thinly sliced
2 cloves of garlic, finely chopped
2 tbsp grated fresh ginger
1 lemongrass stalk, white part only, finely chopped
150g (½ cup) green curry paste
2 x 400ml (14oz) cans coconut cream
1 tbsp brown sugar
4 baby pak choi, halved or quartered
175g (5½oz) Tenderstem broccoli, trimmed

TO SERVE:
mint leaves
lime wedges

1 Preheat a 6-litre (6½-quart) slow cooker on low.
2 Meanwhile, heat the oil in a large frying pan over high heat. Cook the rib pieces on both sides for 5 minutes, or until browned. Transfer to the slow cooker.
3 Add the shallots, garlic, ginger, and lemongrass to the frying pan and cook, stirring, for 1 minute, or until fragrant. Add the curry paste and stir for 1 minute. Add the coconut cream and sugar and stir until well combined. Pour the mixture over the ribs in the slow cooker.
4 Cook, covered, on low for 9 hours, or until the meat is tender.
5 Place the pak choi and broccoli over the ribs in the slow cooker, and cook, covered, on low for 12 minutes, or until tender.
6 Serve the ribs and vegetables with mint leaves and lime wedges.

TIP Ask your butcher to cut the beef ribs in half so you have 12 rib pieces.

Prep + cook time
10 minutes + 9 hours
15 minutes
Serves 6

PRAWN & SQUID COCONUT HOT POT

4 large, cleaned squid tubes, about 1kg (2¼lb)
1½ tbsp extra virgin olive oil
8 shallots
2 cloves of garlic, crushed
4cm (1½-inch) piece fresh ginger, finely grated
1 tbsp ground cumin
2 tsp ground coriander
1 tsp brown mustard seeds
½ tsp ground turmeric
2 long green chillies, finely chopped
6 makrut lime leaves
2 cups (500ml) fish stock
400ml (14oz) can coconut milk
350g (12oz) peeled raw king prawns, tails intact
2½ tbsp fish sauce
2½ tbsp lime juice

TO SERVE:
rice noodles
coriander leaves

1 Cut half the squid tubes into 3cm- (1¼-inch-) wide rings. Cut the remaining hoods down one side, open out, and pat dry. Score the inside lightly in a criss-cross pattern with a small sharp knife, without cutting all the way through. Cut into 8cm (3¼-inch) pieces.
2 Heat the oil in a large frying pan over medium heat and cook the shallots, stirring, for 4 minutes, or until starting to turn golden. Add the garlic, ginger, spices, and chilli and cook, stirring, for 30 seconds until fragrant. Transfer to a 6-litre (6½-quart) slow cooker.
3 Add the squid pieces, lime leaves, stock, and coconut milk. Cook, covered, on low for 4 hours, or until the squid is very tender.
4 Add the prawns and cook, covered, for a further 5 minutes, or until just cooked. Stir through the fish sauce and lime juice.
5 To serve, heat the rice noodles according to the packet instructions. Divide the noodles among serving bowls, ladle over the hot pot, and top with coriander leaves.

TIP If you have time to peel the prawns you will need to buy 800g (1¾lb) prawns in their shells.

Prep + cook time
15 minutes + 4 hours
5 minutes
Serves 4

WHOLE LAMB SHOULDER ROGAN JOSH

1½ tbsp vegetable oil
1.5kg (3¼lb) lamb shoulder, bone in
2 onions, thinly sliced
4 cloves of garlic, thinly sliced
120g (4oz) fresh ginger, finely grated
2 tbsp tomato purée
12 cardamom pods
12 whole cloves
2 cinnamon sticks
2 tbsp ground coriander
1½ tbsp fennel seeds
1 tbsp ground turmeric
1 tsp ground chilli
2 bay leaves
400g (12¼oz) can diced tomatoes
1 tsp salt flakes

TO SERVE:
steamed basmati rice
Greek yogurt
sliced red chilli
mint leaves
sliced cucumber
lime wedges

1 Heat the oil in a large frying pan over high heat. Cook the lamb, fat-side down, for 5 minutes. Turn, then cook a further 5 minutes, or until browned. Transfer to a 5.5-litre (6-quart) slow cooker.

2 Reduce the frying pan heat to medium. Add the onion and cook, stirring, for 5 minutes, or until softened. Add the garlic and ginger and cook, stirring, for 5 minutes, or until caramelized. Add the tomato purée and spices and cook, stirring, for 2 minutes, or until fragrant. Add the bay leaves, canned tomatoes, salt, and 160ml (⅔ cup) water. Transfer the mixture to the slow cooker.

3 Cook, covered, on low for 8 hours.

4 Remove the bay leaves and whole spices and discard. Shred the lamb into the sauce and discard the bones.

5 Serve the rogan josh on rice, topped with yogurt, chilli, and mint, and with sliced cucumber and lime wedges on the side.

Prep + cook time
25 minutes + 8 hours
Serves 6

BEEF, COCONUT & PEANUT CURRY

60ml (¼ cup) vegetable oil
1kg (2¼lb) chuck steak, cut into 5cm (2-inch) pieces
1 onion, roughly chopped
6 cloves of garlic, bruised
4 long red chillies, roughly chopped
5cm (2-inch) piece fresh ginger, roughly chopped
2 tsp ground coriander
70g (¼ cup) tomato purée
8 makrut lime leaves
85g (¼ cup) tamarind paste
1½ tbsp grated palm sugar
1½ tbsp fish sauce
2 lemongrass stalks, bruised
1 beef stock cube, crumbled
40g (½ cup) desiccated coconut, toasted
salt and freshly ground black pepper

TO SERVE:
steamed jasmine rice
roasted peanuts
coriander leaves

1 Heat 1 tablespoon of the oil in a large frying pan over high heat. Cook half the beef for 4 minutes, or until browned all over. Remove from the pan. Repeat with another 1 tablespoon of oil and the remaining beef. Keep the pan to one side.
2 Blend or process the onion, garlic, chillies, ginger, ground coriander, and tomato purée into a smooth paste.
3 Return the reserved frying pan to medium–high heat and add the remaining oil and the spice paste. Cook for 3 minutes, or until fragrant.
4 Heat a 6-litre (6½-quart) slow cooker on low. Add the spice paste and browned beef, then the lime leaves, tamarind, palm sugar, fish sauce, lemongrass, stock cube, and 180ml (¾ cup) water. Stir and season.
5 Cook, covered, on low for 4 hours 30 minutes.
6 Remove the lime leaves and lemongrass and discard. Stir in the toasted desiccated coconut. Season to taste.
7 Serve the curry on steamed jasmine rice, topped with roasted peanuts and fresh coriander leaves.

**Prep + cook time
20 minutes + 4 hours 30 minutes
Serves 4**

SPICED YOGURT LAMB CURRY

1kg (2¼lb) boneless lamb shoulder, cut into 4cm (1½-inch) pieces
2½ tbsp extra virgin olive oil
2 tsp ground coriander
2 tsp ground cumin
1 tsp kashmiri chilli powder
1 tsp sea salt
¼ tsp freshly ground black pepper
1 large red onion, finely chopped
4 cloves of garlic, finely chopped
4cm (1½-inch) piece fresh ginger, finely grated
2½ tbsp tomato purée
2 bay leaves
16 cardamom pods, bruised
8 whole cloves
2 cinnamon sticks
2 large potatoes, about 600g (1lb 5oz), peeled and cut into 3cm (1¼-inch) pieces
110g (½ cup) Greek yogurt

TO SERVE:
brown rice and quinoa mix
toasted pistachios
flat-leaf parsley leaves

1 Heat a heavy-based frying pan over medium–high heat.

2 Place the lamb in a large bowl, drizzle with the oil, and toss to coat. Sprinkle over the ground spices, salt, and pepper and toss to coat. Add the lamb mixture to the pan and cook, turning halfway, for 5 minutes, or until the lamb is browned.

3 Add the onion, garlic, ginger, and tomato purée and cook, stirring, for 2 minutes, or until fragrant. Stir in 250ml (1 cup) water.

4 Transfer the mixture to a 6-litre (6½-quart) slow cooker with the bay leaves and whole spices. Cook, covered, on low for 4 hours.

5 Skim off some of the fat from the surface of the curry and stir in the chopped potatoes. Cook, covered, on low for a further 2 hours.

6 Remove the bay leaves and whole spices from the curry and discard. Stir in the yogurt.

7 Serve the curry on heated brown rice and quinoa mix, topped with toasted pistachios and fresh parsley.

Prep + cook time
15 minutes + 6 hours
Serves 4

JAPANESE BEEF CURRY

2½ tbsp vegetable oil
1kg (2¼lb) stewing beef, cut into 4cm (1½-inch) pieces
1 onion, roughly chopped
3 carrots, cut into 3cm (1¼-inch) pieces
2 potatoes, about 400g (14oz), peeled and cut into 3cm (1¼-inch) pieces
1 tsp hot chilli flakes (optional)
250ml (1 cup) reduced-salt beef stock
92g (3oz) mild Japanese curry mix (see tip)

PICKLED RADISH:
60ml (¼ cup) rice vinegar
1½ tbsp caster sugar
8 radishes, very thinly sliced

SESAME SPINACH:
250g (9oz) baby spinach leaves
2½ tbsp sesame seeds, toasted
2½ tbsp mirin
2 tsp soy sauce
2 tsp caster sugar
salt and freshly ground black pepper

TO SERVE:
steamed sushi rice

1 Heat half the oil in a large frying pan over high heat. Add half the beef and half the onion and cook, turning occasionally, for 3 minutes until browned all over. Transfer to a 6-litre (6½-quart) slow cooker. Repeat with the remaining oil, beef, and onion.

2 Set the slow cooker to low. Add the carrots, potatoes, chilli flakes, stock, and 250ml (1 cup) water. Stir to combine. Cook, covered, on low for 6 hours.

3 When the curry has 15 minutes left, make the pickled radish and sesame spinach. For the pickled radish, put the vinegar, sugar, and 60ml (¼ cup) water in a large jug and stir until the sugar dissolves. Add the radishes and stir to combine.

4 For the sesame spinach, microwave the spinach in a glass bowl on medium for 2 minutes or until just wilted. Combine the sesame seeds, mirin, soy sauce, and sugar in a small bowl, then pour over the spinach. Season to taste.

5 Pour the cooking liquid from the slow cooker into a large microwave-safe jug; you will need 625ml (2½ cups). Add the curry mix to the jug and microwave on high for 2 minutes. Whisk until thick and smooth. Pour the sauce back into the slow cooker and stir through the meat and vegetables.

6 Drain the pickled radish.

7 Serve the curry on sushi rice with the pickled radish and sesame spinach.

TIP Look for golden curry mix with mild spicing, which is available from most supermarkets.

Prep + cook time
15 minutes + 6 hours
5 minutes
Serves 4

'ROAST' CHICKEN KORMA WITH COCONUT RICE STUFFING & CAULIFLOWER

- 250g (9oz) pouch microwavable basmati rice
- 20g (¼ cup) toasted shredded coconut
- 1½ tbsp lime pickle, roughly chopped
- 2½ tbsp sultanas
- 1½ tbsp grated fresh ginger
- 2 tsp garam masala
- 1½ tbsp finely chopped coriander stems, plus leaves to serve
- 1.8kg (3½lb) whole chicken
- 225g (¾ cup) korma paste
- 1 cinnamon stick
- 4 cardamom pods
- 400ml (14oz) can coconut milk
- 500g (1lb 2oz) cauliflower, cut into florets and leaves reserved

1 Combine the rice, coconut, lime pickle, sultanas, ginger, garam masala, and chopped coriander stems in a bowl and season with salt and pepper.

2 Fill the chicken cavity with the rice mixture and tie the legs together with kitchen string.

3 Brush 2 tablespoons of the korma paste over the chicken.

4 Place the remaining paste in a 4.5-litre (5-quart) slow cooker with the cinnamon, cardamom, coconut milk, and 80ml (⅓ cup) water. Stir to combine. Season with salt and pepper. Place the chicken in the slow cooker.

5 Cook, covered, on low for 4 hours.

6 Carefully remove the chicken, cover loosely with foil, and set aside to rest.

7 Add the cauliflower florets and reserved leaves to the slow cooker. Cook, covered, for 1 hour, or until the cauliflower is tender.

8 Preheat the grill to high. Place the chicken on a foil-lined oven tray. Place under the grill for 6 minutes, or until the chicken is browned and lightly charred.

9 Serve the chicken and cauliflower topped with a few coriander leaves.

Prep + cook time
10 minutes + 5 hours 10 minutes
Serves 4

LAMB SHANK & BEETROOT CURRY

4 large lamb shanks (see tips)
1½ tbsp plain flour
80ml (⅓ cup) vegetable oil
280g (10oz) jar beetroot relish
400g (14oz) can crushed tomatoes
500ml (2 cups) chicken stock
1 bunch red or golden beetroot, about 1.5kg (3¼lb), peeled and quartered (see tips)
4 sprigs of curry leaves
salt and freshly ground black pepper

CURRY PASTE:
1½ tbsp coriander seeds
1½ tbsp cumin seeds
1 tsp fennel seeds
1 long fresh red chilli, seeded and roughly chopped
4 cloves of garlic
5cm (2-inch) piece fresh ginger, roughly chopped
2 shallots, quartered
5 coriander roots, washed well

TO SERVE:
coconut yogurt
naan bread

1 Dust the lamb shanks in the flour, shaking off the excess. Heat half the oil in a large frying pan over medium heat and cook the lamb shanks, turning occasionally, for 4 minutes, or until browned. Transfer to a 6-litre (6½-quart) slow cooker.
2 Process the curry paste ingredients in a small food processor into a fine paste.
3 Add the curry paste to the slow cooker with the beetroot relish, canned tomatoes, and stock. Season with salt and pepper and cook, covered, on low for 5 hours.
4 Add the beetroot to the slow cooker. Cook, covered, for 2 hours, or until the beetroot is tender.
5 Heat the remaining oil in a small frying pan over high heat. Cook the curry leaves, in two batches, for 30 seconds, or until crisp. Drain on kitchen paper.
6 Serve the curry with coconut yogurt, naan bread, and the crisp curry leaves.

TIPS Choose lamb shanks that are approximately 250g (9oz) each. You can use large or baby beetroot for this recipe. If using baby beetroot, halve smaller ones and quarter larger ones.

**Prep + cook time
15 minutes + 7 hours
Serves 4**

CHICKEN LAKSA CURRY

1.5kg (3¼lb) chicken thigh cutlets
1 tsp ground turmeric
2½ tbsp rapeseed oil
1 onion, quartered
6 cloves of garlic, bruised
5cm (2-inch) piece fresh ginger, roughly chopped
85g (¼ cup) tamarind paste
2½ tbsp laksa paste (store-bought or see p61)
1½ tbsp grated palm sugar
35g (¼ cup) macadamia halves
10 makrut lime leaves
180ml (¾ cup) coconut cream
2 potatoes, about 400g (14oz), peeled and roughly chopped
salt and freshly ground black pepper

TO SERVE:
steamed jasmine rice

1 Place the chicken in a large bowl, sprinkle over the turmeric, and turn to coat. Season.
2 Heat 1 tablespoon of the oil in a large frying pan over high heat and cook the chicken, turning occasionally, for 6 minutes, or until golden. Transfer to a 6-litre (6½-quart) slow cooker. Keep the frying pan to one side.
3 Meanwhile, blend or process the onion, garlic, ginger, tamarind, laksa paste, sugar, and macadamias into a smooth paste.
4 Return the frying pan to medium–high heat and add the remaining oil, the spice paste, and 6 lime leaves. Cook, stirring occasionally, for 3 minutes or until fragrant. Add the coconut cream and 375ml (1½ cups) water and stir to combine.
5 Turn the slow cooker to low. Add the potatoes and curry sauce and season. Cook, covered, for 4 hours, or until the chicken is very tender.
6 Remove the centre vein from the remaining lime leaves, roll them up tightly, and shred finely.
7 Serve the curry on steamed jasmine rice, topped with the shredded lime leaves.

Prep + cook time
20 minutes + 4 hours
Serves 4

CASHEW & CAULIFLOWER CURRY

1½ tbsp coconut oil
2 onions, thinly sliced
4 cloves of garlic, crushed
2½ tbsp grated fresh ginger
1½ tbsp garam masala
1½ tbsp tomato purée
1kg (2¼lb) cauliflower, cut into florets
300g (2 cups) roasted cashews
400g (14oz) can cherry tomatoes
400ml (14oz) can coconut cream
1 litre (4 cups) vegetable stock
salt and freshly ground black pepper

TO SERVE:
coriander leaves
roti bread

1 Preheat a 6-litre (6½-quart) slow cooker on high.
2 Melt the coconut oil in the slow cooker. Add the onions, garlic, ginger, and garam masala and cook, stirring occasionally, until lightly fragrant. Stir in the tomato purée.
3 Add the cauliflower and cashews and stir until well coated in the mixture. Add the canned tomatoes, coconut cream, and stock, then season well with salt and pepper.
4 Turn the slow cooker to low and cook, covered, for 5 hours, or until the cauliflower and cashews are tender.
5 Serve topped with coriander leaves and with roti on the side.

**Prep + cook time
15 minutes + 5 hours
Serves 4**

DINNER PARTY DISHES

These are the recipes to pull out when you want to impress guests. Getting everything ready in the slow cooker means less mess when friends arrive. From braised duck legs to confit chicken, these recipes are made for long, slow cooking.

CONFIT CHICKEN & ROOT VEGETABLES

4 chicken legs, about 1.4kg (3lb)
1 tbsp sea salt flakes
500g (1lb 2oz) mini carrots
4 shallots, halved
8 cloves of garlic, unpeeled
4 fresh or dried bay leaves
6 sprigs of thyme
2 sprigs of rosemary
400g (14oz) duck fat, melted
830ml ($3\frac{1}{3}$ cups) extra virgin olive oil
3 beetroot, about 500g (1lb 2oz), cut into 4cm (1½-inch) pieces
2 tsp Dijon mustard
2 tbsp white wine vinegar
1 small radicchio, about 200g (7oz), leaves separated
25g (¼ cup) roasted walnuts, chopped
salt and freshly ground black pepper

1 Rub the chicken all over with the salt. Place the chicken in a 5.5-litre (6-quart) slow cooker, then add the carrots, shallots, garlic, bay leaves, thyme, and rosemary. Pour in the duck fat and 750ml (3 cups) olive oil and add the beetroot. Ensure the ingredients are completely covered with oil. Place a piece of baking paper, cut to size, directly on the surface of the oil.

2 Cook, covered, on low for 3 hours, then turn the slow cooker off and allow to stand for 1 hour.

3 Remove the chicken from the slow cooker. Heat a large frying pan over medium–high heat and cook the chicken, skin-side down, for 6 minutes, or until golden brown.

4 Meanwhile, place a sieve over a large bowl and line it with a fine muslin cloth. Once the oil is cool, strain it through the sieve. Discard the bay leaves, rosemary, and thyme. Set aside the vegetables and garlic cloves. Keep the oil for another use (see tip).

5 Squeeze 2 of the garlic cloves into a large bowl and mash with a fork. Add the mustard, vinegar, and remaining olive oil and whisk to combine. Add the radicchio and walnuts and toss gently to combine. Season to taste.

6 Serve the chicken and vegetables with the salad.

TIP Adding the beetroot to the slow cooker after the oil stops it from bleeding its juices over the chicken. Pour the strained oil into an airtight container or jar and refrigerate. Use it in place of butter or oil for frying and roasting.

Prep + cook time
15 minutes + 3 hours
10 minutes, plus standing
Serves 4

UPSIDE-DOWN LAMB RICE

1kg (2¼lb) lamb neck, cut into 4cm (1½-inch) pieces
1 onion, thickly sliced
8 cloves of garlic, smashed
1½ tbsp baharat (see p142)
1 tsp ground turmeric
2 cinnamon sticks
120g (½ cup) ghee
1 aubergine, thickly sliced lengthways
625ml (2½ cups) chicken stock
360g (2 cups) basmati rice, rinsed
50g (⅓ cup) pine nuts
280g (generous 1 cup) Greek yogurt
2 tsp lemon juice
salt and freshly ground black pepper

TO SERVE:
flat-leaf parsley leaves

1 Combine the lamb, onion, garlic, baharat, turmeric, and cinnamon in a large bowl and season.
2 Heat 2½ tablespoons ghee in a large frying pan over high heat. Cook half the lamb mixture, turning occasionally, for 4 minutes, or until browned all over. Remove from the pan. Repeat with another 2½ tablespoons ghee and the remaining lamb.
3 Heat a 5.5-litre (6-quart) slow cooker on low. Brush 1 tablespoon of the ghee over the base and sides of the slow cooker pot. Layer aubergine slices on the base to cover.
4 Spoon the lamb mixture over the aubergine and add 250ml (1 cup) of the stock. Cook, covered, on low for 4 hours, or until the lamb is tender.
5 Turn the slow cooker to high. Place the rice and remaining stock in a medium saucepan; bring to the boil.
6 Transfer the rice mixture to the slow cooker, pressing it into an even layer. Cover with a tea towel, place the lid on top, then fold the towel up over the lid. Cook, covered, for 1 hour 30 minutes, stirring halfway through. Remove the pot from the slow cooker and press the rice down to compact it. Let it stand for 20 minutes.
7 Meanwhile, cook the pine nuts in the remaining ghee in a small frying pan over medium heat for 2 minutes until golden.
8 Combine the yogurt and lemon juice and season.
9 Run a palette knife around the edge of the rice. Place an upturned oval platter on top and carefully invert. Sprinkle with the pine nuts and parsley. Serve with the yogurt.

**Prep + cook time
15 minutes + 5 hours
30 minutes, plus standing
Serves 6**

BEEF SHIN, BEETROOT & POMEGRANATE SOUP

200g (1 cup) dried haricot beans
1 onion, halved
4 cloves of garlic
2 tsp ground cumin
1 tsp dried chilli flakes
1½ tbsp extra virgin olive oil
500g (1lb 2oz) speck, rind removed, cut into 1cm (½-inch) pieces
2kg (4½lb) beef shin
2½ tbsp tomato purée
500ml (2 cups) pomegranate juice
1 litre (4 cups) beef stock
10 baby beetroot, about 250g (9oz), trimmed and scrubbed, small leaves reserved
salt and freshly ground black pepper

TO SERVE:
crème fraîche
crusty bread

1 Place the beans in a bowl with enough water to cover. Cover with cling film and leave to stand overnight. Drain.
2 Pulse the onion, garlic, ground cumin, and chilli flakes in a food processor until finely chopped.
3 Heat the oil in a large, deep frying pan over medium heat. Add the onion mixture and speck and cook, stirring, for 10 minutes, or until golden. Add the beef and cook for 4 minutes each side, or until browned. Stir in the tomato purée, pomegranate juice, and stock, then bring to the boil. Transfer to a 6-litre (6½-quart) slow cooker.
4 Add the drained beans and beetroot and season. Cook, covered, on low for 4 hours 30 minutes, or until the meat is tender.
5 Shred the meat from the bones; discard the bones.
6 Ladle the soup into bowls, top with crème fraîche and the reserved beetroot leaves, and serve with crusty bread.

TIP You will need to start this recipe 1 day ahead.

**Prep + cook time 15 minutes, plus overnight standing + 4 hours 30 minutes
Serves 4**

CAPONATA-INSPIRED PORK

125ml (½ cup) extra virgin olive oil
1.5kg (3¼lb) pork fillet, cut into 5cm (2-inch) pieces
1 large aubergine, cut into 4cm (1½-inch) pieces
8 shallots
4 celery stalks, chopped
6 large tomatoes, chopped
2½ tbsp tomato purée
65g (⅓ cup) drained baby capers
35g (¼ cup) sultanas
80g (½ cup) green olives
2½ tbsp red wine vinegar
750ml (3 cups) chicken stock
salt and freshly ground black pepper

TO SERVE:
your favourite pasta
finely chopped flat-leaf parsley

1 Heat 1 tablespoon of the oil in a large, deep frying pan over medium heat. Cook the pork, in two batches, for 4 minutes, turning until browned. Transfer to a 6-litre (6½-quart) slow cooker.
2 Heat 80ml (⅓ cup) of the remaining oil in the same frying pan and cook the aubergine for 5 minutes until golden. Transfer to the slow cooker.
3 Cook the shallots and celery in the same frying pan for 4 minutes, or until browned. Transfer to the slow cooker, then add the chopped tomatoes, tomato purée, half the capers, the sultanas, olives, vinegar, and stock. Season. Cook, covered, on low for 6 hours until the meat is tender.
4 Heat the remaining oil in a small frying pan and cook the remaining capers, stirring, for 4 minutes, or until crisp. Drain on kitchen paper.
5 Serve the pork on pasta, topped with the crisp capers and some chopped fresh parsley.

TIP Ziti pasta is used here, but you can use any pasta you prefer.

Prep + cook time
20 minutes + 6 hours
Serves 8

MILK-POACHED WHOLE CHICKEN

1.5kg (3¼lb) whole chicken
120g (1 stick) butter
1 leek, cut into 5cm (2-inch) lengths
8 cloves of garlic
6 sprigs of thyme, leaves picked
2 fresh bay leaves
500ml (2 cups) whole milk
1½ tbsp finely grated lemon zest
1½ tbsp lemon juice
100ml (6½ tbsp) double cream
25g (1¾ tbsp) butter
handful of tarragon leaves
handful of sage leaves
salt and freshly ground black pepper

1 Season the chicken all over. Heat 30g (2 tbsp) of the butter in a large heavy-based saucepan over medium heat. Add the chicken, breast-side down, and cook until lightly browned. Add another 30g (2 tbsp) of butter to the pan, turn the chicken over, and cook until lightly browned. Transfer the chicken, breast-side up, to a 5.5-litre (6-quart) slow cooker and set to low.

2 Place another 30g (2 tbsp) butter in the same saucepan with the leek, garlic, thyme, and bay leaves. Cook, stirring, for 3 minutes until the leek begins to take on colour. Stir in the milk, lemon zest, and lemon juice and bring to a gentle simmer. The milk will curdle.

3 Pour the mixture over the chicken in the slow cooker. Cook, covered, on low for 4 hours.

4 Transfer the chicken and leek pieces to a serving platter and cover to keep warm. Strain the cooking liquid into a saucepan over medium heat and whisk in the cream. Bring to a gentle simmer, then remove from the heat. Season to taste.

5 Heat the remaining 30g (2 tbsp) butter in a small saucepan over medium heat until foaming. Cook the tarragon and sage, stirring, until crisp.

6 Serve the chicken and leek with the sauce, topped with the crisp herbs.

SERVE IT Serve with mashed potatoes or crunchy salad greens.

**Prep + cook time
15 minutes + 4 hours
Serves 4**

CHORIZO, POTATO & WHITE BEAN STEW

2½ tbsp extra virgin olive oil
2 spicy chorizo, about 200g (7oz), cut thickly
125ml (½ cup) dry white wine
500ml (2 cups) chicken stock
1kg (2¼lb) baby potatoes, halved
2 small red onions, cut into wedges
3 carrots, cut into 4cm (1½-inch) pieces
3 celery stalks, cut into 4cm (1½-inch) pieces
2 sprigs of rosemary
1 fresh or dried bay leaf
400g (14oz) can cannellini beans, drained and rinsed
1 bunch cavolo nero, about 300g (10½oz), chopped
salt and freshly ground black pepper

ALMOND ROMESCO:
200g (7oz) drained roasted piquillo peppers
80ml (⅓ cup) extra virgin olive oil
50g (1¾oz) roasted almonds
2½ tbsp sherry vinegar
1 tsp smoked paprika
1 small clove of garlic, crushed

1 Heat the oil in a large frying pan over medium–high heat. Cook the chorizo, stirring occasionally, for 3 minutes, or until golden. Transfer to a 5.5-litre (6-quart) slow cooker.
2 Add the wine to the same frying pan and simmer for 2 minutes, or until reduced by half. Add the stock and bring to a simmer. Pour the stock mixture into the slow cooker, then add the potatoes, onions, carrots, celery, rosemary, and bay leaf. Cook, covered, on low for 4 hours.
3 Add the beans and cavolo nero and stir to combine. Cook, covered, on low for a further 30 minutes. Season to taste.
4 Make the almond romesco by blending the ingredients in a high-speed blender until smooth. Season to taste.
5 Serve the stew topped with the romesco.

Prep + cook time
15 minutes + 4 hours 30 minutes
Serves 4

LAMB NECK WITH ROSEMARY & PRESERVED LEMON

3½ tbsp extra virgin olive oil
4 x 350g (12oz) lamb necks
2 large onions, chopped
4 sprigs of rosemary
350g (12oz) jar preserved lemons, drained, flesh removed, and rind thinly sliced
750ml (3 cups) chicken stock
2 fennel bulbs, trimmed and quartered (fronds reserved to serve)
salt and freshly ground black pepper

TO SERVE:
steamed couscous

1 Preheat a 5.5-litre (6-quart) slow cooker on high.
2 Heat 2 tbsp oil in a large frying pan over medium–high heat. Cook the lamb, turning regularly, until browned all over. Transfer to the slow cooker.
3 Cook the onions in the same frying pan, stirring, for 5 minutes, or until lightly golden. Transfer to the slow cooker, then add the rosemary, preserved lemon rind, and stock. Adjust the slow cooker setting to low and cook, covered, for 9 hours 30 minutes, or until the meat is very tender.
4 When the lamb has 30 minutes left in the slow cooker, preheat the oven to 200°C (180°C fan/400°F/Gas 6).
5 Toss the fennel in the remaining oil on a large oven tray lined with baking paper and season. Roast for 20 minutes, or until golden and tender.
6 Remove the lamb from the slow cooker and cover to keep warm. Strain the cooking liquid into a saucepan over medium heat and bring to the boil. Cook until reduced by half.
7 Serve the lamb with the roasted fennel and couscous, drizzled with the sauce. Sprinkle with the reserved fennel fronds.

Prep + cook time
15 minutes + 9 hours
35 minutes
Serves 6

HONEY BALSAMIC PORK BELLY

---

2 red onions
1.2kg (2½lb) boneless pork belly, rind on
2 tsp sea salt flakes
90g (¼ cup) honey
1 clove of garlic, crushed
60ml (¼ cup) balsamic vinegar
1½ tbsp extra virgin olive oil
1 small radicchio, about 200g (7oz), thickly shredded
3 large ripe figs, sliced
300g (10½oz) green beans, trimmed and blanched
handful of small basil leaves

1 Cut the red onions into 2cm- (¾-inch-) thick wedges and arrange over the base of a 4.5-litre (5-quart) slow cooker.
2 Using a sharp knife, score the pork rind at 1cm (½-inch) intervals and rub salt flakes all over. Place the pork, rind-side up, on the onions.
3 Whisk the honey, garlic, and vinegar in a small jug and pour over the pork. Cook, covered, on low for 6 hours.
4 Remove the pork, then the onions, with a slotted spoon.
5 Heat the oil in a large frying pan over medium–high heat. Add the pork, rind-side down, then arrange the onions around the pork. Cook for 2 minutes, or until the rind is golden and crisp and the edges of the onions begin to crisp.
6 Remove the pork, loosely cover with foil, and set aside to rest.
7 Meanwhile, pour the cooking liquid into a large saucepan over high heat and bring to the boil. Cook until reduced by half.
8 Cut the pork belly into thick slices. Serve the pork and onions with the radicchio, figs, and beans. Drizzle with the sauce and top with basil leaves.

Prep + cook time
15 minutes + 6 hours
10 minutes
Serves 6

SALT 'BAKED' TROUT WITH HERBY POTATOES

500g (1lb 2oz) baby potatoes, cut into 5mm (¼-inch) slices
20g (1½ tbsp) butter
1 shallot, finely chopped
1 clove of garlic, crushed
1 lemon
3 sprigs of dill
3 sprigs of tarragon
2 small whole rainbow trout, about 600g (1lb 5oz), cleaned (see tip)
1kg (2¼lb) rock salt
2 egg whites, lightly beaten
1 tsp Dijon mustard
235g (1 cup) crème fraîche
125g (4oz) watercress leaves
salt and freshly ground black pepper

1 Layer the potato slices over the base of a 4.5-litre (5-quart) slow cooker.
2 Melt the butter in a large frying pan over medium heat and cook the shallot and garlic, stirring, until softened. Pour over the potatoes in the slow cooker, then add 125ml (½ cup) water.
3 Thinly slice half the lemon and place the lemon slices and a sprig each of dill and tarragon into the cavity of each fish.
4 Stir the rock salt and egg whites in a large bowl until a thick paste forms.
5 Layer two sheets of foil, large enough to enclose both fish, and top with a sheet of baking paper, leaving a 2cm (¾-inch) border. Scoop half the salt mixture onto one side of the paper. Place both fish on top, then cover with the remaining salt mixture. Fold up the foil and paper to enclose the fish. Roll up the sides tightly to seal.
6 Place the parcel on the potatoes in the slow cooker. Cook, covered, on low for 4 hours. Remove the parcel from the slow cooker. Rest for 5 minutes.
7 Meanwhile, drain the potatoes. Roughly chop the remaining dill and tarragon. Stir the herbs and mustard through the potatoes. Season to taste.
8 Finely grate the zest of the remaining lemon half into a bowl, then squeeze the juice into the bowl. Gently whisk in the crème fraîche and season.
9 Unwrap the fish parcel. Crack the salt crust and peel off the salt and fish skin. Serve with the herby potatoes, watercress, and lemon crème fraîche.

TIP If the whole fish don't fit in your slow cooker, remove the heads before wrapping in the parcel.

**Prep + cook time
15 minutes + 4 hours
Serves 4**

RED WINE-BRAISED BEEF RIBS WITH MUSHROOMS

15g (½oz) dried porcini mushrooms
2½ tbsp extra virgin olive oil
12 beef short ribs, about 3kg (6¾lb)
6 shallots
4 cloves of garlic, thinly sliced
400g (14oz) chestnut mushrooms
125ml (½ cup) red wine
125ml (½ cup) port
100g (3½oz) pancetta
8 sprigs of thyme, plus extra to serve
2 fresh or dried bay leaves
375ml (1½ cups) beef stock
2 tsp sherry vinegar
salt and freshly ground black pepper

TO SERVE:
mashed potatoes
flat-leaf parsley leaves

1 Place the porcini in a small bowl with 250ml (1 cup) boiling water.
2 Heat 1 tablespoon of the oil in a large frying pan over medium–high heat. Season the ribs all over. Cook the ribs, in batches, turning, for 6 minutes, or until browned on both sides. Transfer the ribs to a 5.5-litre (6-quart) slow cooker.
3 Heat the remaining oil in the same frying pan and cook the shallots, garlic, and chestnut mushrooms, stirring occasionally, for 5 minutes until browned. Add the wine and port and simmer for 2 minutes, or until reduced by half. Add the pancetta, porcini and soaking liquid, thyme, bay leaves, and stock.
4 Transfer the mixture to the slow cooker and cook, covered, on low for 8 hours.
5 Remove the ribs from the slow cooker and cover to keep warm. Strain the cooking liquid into a large frying pan over medium heat (discard the solids). Bring to the boil, then reduce the heat and simmer for 8 minutes, or until thickened. Stir in the vinegar. Season to taste.
6 Serve the ribs on mashed potatoes, drizzled with the sauce. Top with parsley and extra thyme.

Prep + cook time
20 minutes + 8 hours
10 minutes
Serves 6

BRAISED DUCK LEGS IN JUNIPER & THYME

---

8 duck legs, about 1.5kg (3¼lb)
2 bulbs of garlic, halved horizontally
6 sprigs of thyme
2 tsp juniper berries
1 mandarin, peeled, rind thinly sliced, and segments separated
750ml (3 cups) warm chicken stock
1 large celeriac, peeled and cut into wedges
2½ tbsp extra virgin olive oil
salt and freshly ground black pepper

TO SERVE:
finely chopped flat-leaf parsley

1 Preheat a 5.5-litre (6-quart) slow cooker on high.
2 Heat a large frying pan over medium–high heat. Cook the duck, skin-side down, until the fat begins to render, then turn over and cook the other side until the duck is golden all over.
3 Transfer the duck to the slow cooker, then add the garlic, thyme, juniper berries, mandarin rind and segments, and the stock. Turn the slow cooker to low and cook, covered, for 6 hours 30 minutes until the duck is very tender.
4 When the duck has 1 hour left in the cooker, preheat the oven to 180°C (160°C fan/350°F/Gas 4) and line a large oven tray with baking paper.
5 Toss the celeriac in the oil and arrange on the lined tray. Season. Roast for 45 minutes, or until golden and tender.
6 Transfer the duck and 3 of the garlic bulb halves to a large oven tray.
7 Strain the cooking liquid into a saucepan over medium heat and squeeze the garlic from the remaining bulb half into the pan. Blend until smooth using a stick blender, then bring to the boil. Cook for 6 minutes, or until the sauce is slightly thickened.
8 Meanwhile, preheat the grill to high. Place the duck and garlic under the grill until browned and crisp.
9 Serve the duck, roasted celeriac, and garlic, drizzled with sauce and sprinkled with parsley.

Prep + cook time
15 minutes + 6 hours
40 minutes
Serves 4

SUMAC & ONION-BRAISED BEEF CHEEKS

2½ tbsp extra virgin olive oil
6 beef cheeks, about 1.4kg (3lb)
280g (10oz) jar caramelized onions
4 cloves of garlic, crushed
400g (14oz) can crushed tomatoes
80ml (⅓ cup) pomegranate molasses
285g (10oz) jar piquillo peppers
   (including the liquid)
2½ tbsp sumac, plus extra to serve
520g (2 cups) store-bought hummus
handful of small flat-leaf
   parsley leaves
handful of small mint leaves
seeds of 1 pomegranate
1 small red onion, thinly sliced
1½ tbsp lemon juice
salt and freshly ground black pepper

1 Preheat a 4.5-litre (5-quart) slow cooker on low.

2 Heat the oil in a large non-stick frying pan over high heat. Season the beef, then add to the pan and cook, turning occasionally, for 6 minutes, or until browned.

3 Transfer the beef to the slow cooker, then add the caramelized onions, garlic, canned tomatoes, pomegranate molasses, peppers and their liquid, the sumac, and 250ml (1 cup) water. Season. Cook, covered, for 7 hours, or until the beef is very tender.

4 Carefully remove the beef and cover to keep warm. Strain the cooking liquid into a saucepan over high heat. Bring to the boil, then simmer for 6 minutes, or until reduced by a third.

5 Meanwhile, place the hummus in a saucepan with 60ml (¼ cup) water over medium heat. Cook, stirring, for 2 minutes, or until just warmed through.

6 Place the parsley, mint, pomegranate seeds, red onion, and lemon juice in a bowl and season. Toss gently to combine.

7 Spoon the warm hummus onto serving plates, top with the beef and pan juices, and sprinkle with extra sumac. Serve with the herb salad.

SERVE IT Serve with Afghan flatbread or Turkish pide.

Prep + cook time
15 minutes + 7 hours
10 minutes
Serves 6

SLOW-COOKED PORK LETTUCE WRAPS

4 spring onions, chopped
4 cloves of garlic
4cm (1½-inch) piece fresh ginger, chopped
60ml (¼ cup) sesame oil
2½ tbsp soy sauce
1½ tbsp caster sugar
1 tsp ground white pepper
1.5kg (3¼lb) boneless pork neck

TO SERVE:
oak lettuce leaves
steamed sushi rice
kimchi
gochujang (Korean chilli paste)
sliced spring onions
toasted sesame seeds

1 Process the spring onions, garlic, ginger, sesame oil, soy sauce, sugar, and white pepper in a small food processor until a fine paste forms.
2 Layer three large sheets of foil on top of one another. Rub the paste all over the pork, then place in the centre of the foil and wrap tightly. Place the pork parcel in a 4.5-litre (5-quart) slow cooker with 250ml (1 cup) water. Cook, covered, on low for 7 hours.
3 Preheat the grill to high.
4 Remove the pork from the slow cooker and unwrap it so the top of the pork is exposed. Place on a large oven tray, then grill for 5 minutes, or until the pork is charred. Shred the pork using two forks.
5 To serve, place the shredded pork on lettuce leaves with sushi rice, then top with kimchi, gochujang, sliced spring onions, and sesame seeds.

Prep + cook time
10 minutes + 7 hours
5 minutes
Serves 4–6

MOJO PORK ROLLS

6 soft long white bread rolls, halved lengthways
95g (⅓ cup) Dijon mustard
12 slices of ham
12 slices of Swiss cheese
120g (½ cup) pickled cucumber
softened butter, for spreading
salt and freshly ground black pepper

MOJO PORK:
1.2kg (2½lb) boneless pork shoulder
4 tbsp finely grated orange zest
180ml (¾ cup) orange juice
1½ tbsp finely grated lime zest
60ml (¼ cup) lime juice
4 cloves of garlic, crushed
2 tsp ground cumin
large handful of coriander, finely chopped
small handful of mint leaves, finely chopped

TO SERVE:
crisps

1 For the mojo pork, place the pork in a large zip-lock bag with all the other ingredients and season generously. Seal the bag and gently shake the bag until very well combined. Refrigerate overnight.
2 Transfer the pork and marinade to a 5.5-litre (6-quart) slow cooker. Cook, covered, on low for 8 hours.
3 Preheat the grill to high.
4 Remove the pork from the slow cooker and place on a large oven tray. Grill for 10 minutes, or until the pork is browned. Shred the pork into large pieces.
5 To assemble, spread the cut sides of each roll with mustard. Divide the ham, shredded pork, cheese, and pickles among the rolls.
6 Spread butter on the outside of the rolls. Cook in a preheated panini press (or in a frying pan, cooking on both sides) until golden brown and the cheese is melted.
7 Serve the rolls cut in half, with crisps.

TIPS You need to start this recipe 1 day ahead. You will need 3 oranges and 2 limes for this recipe.

**Prep + cook time 15 minutes, plus overnight chilling + 8 hours 10 minutes
Serves 6**

'CLAY POT' CHICKEN RICE

1½ tbsp sesame oil
360g (2 cups) jasmine rice, rinsed
4 boneless chicken thighs, about 600g (1lb 5oz), cut into 3cm (1¼-inch) pieces
2 lup cheong (sweet Chinese sausage), about 60g (2oz), thinly sliced
100g (3½oz) shiitake mushrooms, sliced
60ml (¼ cup) light soy sauce
60ml (¼ cup) dark soy sauce
1½ tbsp honey
¼ tsp ground white pepper

TO SERVE:
shredded spring onions
lime wedges

1 Preheat a 5.5-litre (6-quart) slow cooker to high.

2 Heat the sesame oil in a large frying pan over high heat. Add the rice and cook, stirring, for 5 minutes, or until fragrant and lightly toasted. Transfer to the slow cooker, then add the chicken, sausages, mushrooms, and 500ml (2 cups) water.

3 Combine the soy sauces, honey, and white pepper in a small jug. Pour over the mixture in the slow cooker. Cover the slow cooker with a clean tea towel, place the lid on top, then fold the towel over the lid. Turn the heat to low and cook for 4 hours.

4 Stir the rice mixture before spooning it into serving bowls. Top with shredded spring onion and serve with lime wedges.

Prep + cook time
15 minutes + 4 hours
Serves 4

BATCH COOKING

Cooking large portions in your slow cooker is the ideal way to fill your freezer with nutritious meals to whip out when you need them. Batch cooking is a time- and cost-effective way of preparing food – simply pop all your ingredients in and let the slow cooker do the work.

SLOW COOKER PASTITSIO

1½ tbsp olive oil
2 onions, chopped
2 cloves of garlic, crushed
1 tsp chilli flakes
1 tsp ground cinnamon
½ tsp ground nutmeg
1kg (2¼lb) minced lamb
160ml (⅔ cup) red wine
810ml (3¼ cups) tomato passata
2½ tbsp tomato purée
500g (1lb 2oz) rigatoni
50g (½ cup) grated mozzarella
40g (½ cup) grated Parmesan
salt and freshly ground black pepper

RICOTTA TOPPING:
750g (1lb 10oz) ricotta, crumbled
180ml (¾ cup) single cream
2 egg yolks

TO SERVE:
green salad

1 Heat the oil in a large, deep frying pan over medium–high heat and cook the onion, stirring, for 3 minutes, or until softened. Add the garlic, chilli flakes, cinnamon, and half the nutmeg, then cook, stirring, for 30 seconds, or until fragrant. Add the lamb and cook, stirring to break up any lumps, for 5 minutes, or until browned. Add the wine and bring to the boil, then reduce the heat and simmer for 3 minutes, or until the liquid has almost evaporated. Stir in the passata and tomato purée and season.

2 Remove the pot from a 6-litre (6½-quart) slow cooker and line the base with baking paper. Spoon half the lamb mixture over the base and arrange the pasta on top. Cover with the remaining lamb mixture. Return the pot to the slow cooker.

3 Whisk the ricotta ingredients together in a large bowl until smooth, then season to taste. Spread the ricotta topping over the lamb and sprinkle with the remaining nutmeg. Place a piece of baking paper (cut to size) directly on the topping. Cook, covered, on low for 3 hours 50 minutes, or until the topping is set.

4 Preheat the grill to high.

5 Remove the pot from the slow cooker. Remove the baking paper and top with the cheeses. Grill for 5 minutes, or until the cheeses are golden and melted. Let it stand for 15 minutes before slicing.

6 Serve the pastitsio with a green salad.

**Prep + cook time
15 minutes + 4 hours,
plus standing
Serves 8**

PORK, APPLE & FENNEL STEW

2½ tbsp olive oil
2kg (4½lb) boneless pork shoulder, skin removed, halved lengthways
1 onion, roughly chopped
2 celery stalks, cut into 4cm (1½-inch) lengths
2 fennel bulbs, cut into wedges
2 cloves of garlic, crushed
½ tsp chilli flakes
2½ tbsp plain flour
125ml (½ cup) white wine
750ml (3 cups) chicken stock
5 sprigs of thyme, plus extra to serve
4 red apples, cut into wedges
salt and freshly ground black pepper

TO SERVE:
crusty bread

1 Heat half the oil in a large frying pan over high heat. Season the pork, then add to the pan and cook for 3 minutes on each side, or until browned all over. Transfer to a 6-litre (6½-quart) slow cooker.

2 Heat the remaining oil in the same frying pan over medium–high heat and cook the onion, celery, and fennel, stirring occasionally, for 3 minutes, or until browned. Stir in the garlic and chilli flakes and cook for 30 seconds, or until fragrant. Add the flour and wine and bring to the boil, then reduce the heat and simmer for 3 minutes, or until the liquid has almost evaporated.

3 Carefully transfer to the slow cooker. Add the stock and thyme, then season. Cook, covered, on low for 4 hours, or until the pork is just tender.

4 Add the apples to the slow cooker and cook, covered, for a further 1 hour, or until the pork is falling apart and the apples are tender. Season.

5 Serve the stew topped with extra thyme and with crusty bread.

**Prep + cook time
15 minutes + 5 hours
Serves 8**

FIVE-SPICE BRAISED SALT BEEF

2.25kg (5lb) piece of salt beef
2½ tbsp olive oil
2 cloves of garlic, crushed
2cm (¾-inch) piece fresh ginger, grated
10 spring onions, cut into 5cm (2-inch) lengths, plus extra, shredded, to serve
handful of chopped coriander stems
2 tsp Chinese five spice
1 tsp chilli flakes
500ml (2 cups) beef stock
80ml (⅓ cup) hoisin sauce
60ml (¼ cup) Chinese cooking wine (shaohsing)
1½ tbsp rice wine vinegar
4 baby pak choi, halved lengthways
2½ tbsp brown sugar
salt and freshly ground black pepper

TO SERVE:
lime wedges

1 Place the salt beef in a large bowl with enough water to cover. Cover and refrigerate overnight.
2 The next day, drain the beef and pat dry with kitchen paper.
3 Heat half the oil in a large, deep frying pan over medium–high heat. Cook the beef, turning, for 5 minutes, or until browned all over, then transfer to a 6-litre (6½-quart) slow cooker.
4 Heat the remaining oil in the same frying pan and cook the garlic, ginger, spring onions, and coriander stems, stirring, for 3 minutes, or until the onions soften. Add the five spice and chilli flakes and cook, stirring, for 30 seconds, or until fragrant. Add the stock, hoisin, cooking wine, and vinegar and bring to the boil. Season, then carefully pour over the beef in the slow cooker.
5 Cook, covered, on low for 4 hours, or until the beef is tender.
6 Add the pak choi to the slow cooker. Cook, covered, for 5 minutes, or until the leaves just start to wilt. Carefully remove the pak choi and beef from the slow cooker and cover to keep warm.
7 Strain the cooking liquid into a saucepan over high heat. Stir in the sugar and bring to the boil. Reduce the heat to low and simmer for 20 minutes, or until reduced slightly.
8 To serve, slice the beef and serve with the reduced liquid and pak choi, topped with extra shredded spring onions and lime wedges.

TIP You need to start this recipe 1 day ahead.

**Prep + cook time 15 minutes, plus overnight chilling + 4 hours 25 minutes
Serves 8**

PORK, BARLEY & KALE STEW

1½ tbsp olive oil
1kg (2¼lb) American-style pork spare ribs
30g (2 tbsp) butter, chopped
1 onion, thinly sliced
6 cloves of garlic, bruised
3 bay leaves
2 potatoes, about 400g (14oz), roughly chopped
150g (¾ cup) pearl barley
1.25 litres (5 cups) chicken stock
300g (10½oz) kale, torn and stalks removed
2 tsp chopped dill, plus extra to serve
salt and freshly ground black pepper

TO SERVE:
crusty bread

1 Heat the oil in a large, deep frying pan over high heat. Season the ribs well, then cook the ribs, in batches, turning for 3 minutes, or until golden. Transfer to a 5-litre (5-quart) slow cooker.
2 Melt the butter in the same frying pan over medium–high heat. Cook the onion, garlic, and bay leaves, stirring, for 3 minutes, or until the onion softens. Transfer to the slow cooker, then add the potatoes, barley, and stock. Stir to combine, then season.
3 Cook, covered, on low for 4 hours 30 minutes, or until the meat is falling off the bone.
4 Adjust the cooker setting to high. Add the kale and dill and stir to combine. Cook, covered, for a further 30 minutes, then season.
5 Serve the stew topped with extra dill sprigs and crusty bread.

Prep + cook time
15 minutes + 5 hours
Serves 4

SHREDDED BEEF & MUSHROOM POT PIES

75g (½ cup) plain flour
1.2kg (2½lb) piece of beef brisket, trimmed
2½ tbsp olive oil
2½ tbsp tomato purée
250ml (1 cup) dry red wine
400g (14oz) portobello mushrooms, roughly chopped
1 large onion, roughly chopped
1 large carrot, roughly chopped
60ml (¼ cup) caramelized balsamic vinegar
3 cloves of garlic, crushed
7 sprigs of rosemary
2 sheets of all-butter puff pastry
1 egg, lightly beaten
salt and freshly ground black pepper

1 Place the flour in a large bowl and season. Add the beef and toss to coat.
2 Heat the oil in a large frying pan over high heat. Cook the beef for 10 minutes until browned. Cut the beef into six pieces and place in a 4.5-litre (5-quart) slow cooker. Keep the juices in the pan.
3 Add any leftover flour and the tomato purée to the juices in the pan and cook, stirring, for 1 minute until thickened. Add the wine and 750ml (3 cups) water. Cook, stirring, until smooth. Bring to the boil, then pour over the beef. Add the mushrooms, onion, carrot, vinegar, garlic, and 1 rosemary sprig and stir.
4 Cook, covered, on low for 8 hours, or until the beef is tender. Discard the rosemary sprig.
5 Remove the beef from the slow cooker and shred it coarsely using two forks. Return to the slow cooker, season, and stir.
6 Spread the mixture on a baking tray, cover, and refrigerate until cold.
7 Preheat the oven to 200°C (180°C fan/400°F/Gas 6) and lightly oil six 430ml (1¾-cup) ramekins.
8 Using a ramekin as a guide, cut six rounds from the pastry. Spoon the beef mixture into the ramekins and place a pastry round on top. Press with a fork to seal the edges. Brush with egg, pierce a hole in the centre, and insert a sprig of rosemary into each hole. Sprinkle with salt.
9 Place the ramekins on an oven tray and bake for 25 minutes until the pastry is golden and puffed.

KEEP IT Freeze the filling for up to 2 months. Defrost and continue from step 7.

Prep + cook time
15 minutes + 8 hours
30 minutes, plus chilling
Serves 6

BRAISED LAMB SHANKS WITH BEANS & FETA

2½ tbsp olive oil
8 French-trimmed lamb shanks, about 2kg (4½lb)
2 onions, thinly sliced
6 cloves of garlic, crushed
90g (⅓ cup) tomato purée
160ml (⅔ cup) white wine
2 x 400g (14oz) cans crushed tomatoes
8 sprigs of thyme
2 cinnamon sticks
4 cloves
2 fresh bay leaves
125ml (½ cup) chicken stock
2 tsp malt vinegar
300g (10½oz) green beans, trimmed
handful of dill, chopped, plus extra sprigs to serve
100g (3½oz) feta, crumbled
salt and freshly ground black pepper

TO SERVE:
orzo

1 Heat half the oil in a large frying pan over medium–high heat. Season the lamb shanks, then cook, in batches, turning, for 6 minutes or until browned all over. Transfer to a 5.5-litre (6-quart) slow cooker.

2 Heat the remaining oil in the same frying pan. Cook the onions, stirring, for 7 minutes, or until golden. Add the garlic and tomato purée and cook, stirring, for 2 minutes, or until fragrant. Add the wine, bring to the boil, then reduce the heat and simmer for 2 minutes, or until reduced by half.

3 Add to the slow cooker along with the canned tomatoes, thyme, cinnamon, cloves, bay leaves, chicken stock, and vinegar. Season and stir to combine.

4 Cook, covered, on low for 6 hours.

5 Add the beans and cook, covered, for 2 hours, or until the shanks are very tender. Remove the bay leaves and whole spices and discard. Stir through the dill.

6 Serve the lamb shanks topped with feta and extra dill on orzo.

**Prep + cook time
20 minutes + 8 hours
Serves 8**

COURGETTE & CHORIZO CORNBREAD SLICE

75g (½ cup) self-raising flour
85g (½ cup) instant polenta
2 courgettes, coarsely grated
1 corn cob, kernels cut off
50g (1¾oz) chorizo, roughly chopped (see tips)
2 spring onions, thinly sliced
90g (¾ cup) coarsely grated Cheddar
8 eggs
180g (¾ cup) sour cream
salt and freshly ground black pepper

TO SERVE (OPTIONAL):
salad leaves
tomato relish

1 Oil the pot of a 4.5-litre (5-quart) slow cooker. Line the base and long sides, allowing the baking paper to come halfway up the sides.
2 Combine the flour, polenta, courgettes, corn kernels, and half the chorizo, half the spring onions, and half the cheese in a large bowl. Whisk the eggs and sour cream in a large jug, then add to the flour mixture in the bowl. Season and stir until just combined.
3 Pour the mixture into the slow cooker and smooth the surface. Scatter evenly with the remaining chorizo, spring onion, and cheese. Cook, covered, on low for 4 hours, or until a skewer inserted into the centre comes out clean.
4 Remove the lid, cover the slow cooker with a clean tea towel, and place the lid on top. Leave to cool.
5 Using the baking paper, carefully lift the cornbread out of the slow cooker and transfer top-side-up to a chopping board, then cut into slices.
6 Serve the cornbread with salad leaves and tomato relish, if liked.

TIPS Swap the chorizo for the same amount of pancetta, prosciutto, or salami, if you prefer. Cornbread slice will keep refrigerated in an airtight container for up to 3 days.

Prep + cook time
15 minutes + 4 hours, plus cooling
Serves 8

SMOKY MUSHROOM SOUP WITH GARLIC YOGURT

80ml (⅓ cup) olive oil
1 large onion, roughly chopped
1 celery stalk, roughly chopped
1 large carrot, roughly chopped
1 bird's eye chilli, seeded and finely chopped
2 tsp thyme leaves, plus extra to serve
2 fresh bay leaves
1½ tbsp smoked paprika
60ml (¼ cup) sweet sherry
800g (1¾lb) chestnut mushrooms
2 potatoes, about 600g (1lb 5oz), cut into 1cm (½-inch) pieces
1 litre (4 cups) vegetable stock
salt and freshly ground black pepper

GARLIC YOGURT:
2 cups (560g) natural yogurt
1 tsp salt
1 clove of garlic, crushed

TO SERVE:
crusty bread

1 For the garlic yogurt, place a sieve over a bowl and line with muslin. Combine the yogurt, salt, and garlic in a separate bowl, then spoon into the muslin. Gather into a ball, secure with string or an elastic band, and chill for 5 hours, or until thickened. Transfer to a small airtight container and refrigerate until needed.

2 Preheat a 5.5-litre (6-quart) slow cooker on high.

3 Heat 60ml (¼ cup) of the oil in a large frying pan over medium–high heat. Cook the onion, celery, and carrot, stirring, for 5 minutes until softened. Add the chilli, thyme, bay leaves, and paprika and cook, stirring, for 1 minute, or until fragrant. Add the sherry and bring to the boil. Carefully add the mixture to the slow cooker.

4 Roughly chop 700g (1½lb) of the mushrooms and thickly slice the rest.

5 Turn the slow cooker to low. Add the chopped mushrooms, potatoes, and stock and stir to combine. Cook, covered, on low for 5 hours 30 minutes. Discard the bay leaves.

6 When there is 5 minutes left, heat the remaining oil in the same frying pan over medium–high heat. Cook the sliced mushrooms for 4 minutes, or until golden.

7 Using a stick blender, blend the soup until smooth. Season to taste.

8 Ladle the soup into bowls and top with yogurt, fried mushrooms, extra thyme, and black pepper. Serve with crusty bread.

KEEP IT This soup is suitable for freezing after blending. Allow it to defrost before reheating. You could freeze it in portions.

Prep + cook time
15 minutes, plus chilling
+ 5 hours 30 minutes
Serves 6–8

FRENCH-STYLE CHICKEN LEGS

6 chicken legs, about 2kg (4½lb)
50g (3½ tbsp) butter, chopped
150g (5¼oz) piece of speck,
 cut into batons
4 cloves of garlic, thinly sliced
2½ tbsp plain flour
250ml (1 cup) white wine
250ml (1 cup) chicken stock
8 shallots
2 carrots, thickly sliced
200g (7oz) chestnut mushrooms,
 larger ones halved
salt and freshly ground black pepper

TO SERVE (OPTIONAL):
tarragon leaves

1 Preheat a 6.5-litre (7-quart) slow cooker on high.
2 Heat a large non-stick frying pan over high heat. Season the chicken, then cook it, in batches, for 3 minutes on each side, or until browned all over. Transfer the chicken to the slow cooker.
3 Melt the butter in the same frying pan over medium heat and cook the speck, stirring, for 5 minutes, or until golden. Add the garlic and cook for 1 minute, or until fragrant. Stir in the flour and cook, stirring continuously, for 1 minute. Increase the heat to high, add the wine and stock, and bring to the boil.
4 Carefully pour over the chicken in the slow cooker and top with the shallots and carrots, then stir to combine.
5 Adjust the slow cooker setting to low and cook, covered, for 4 hours.
6 Add the mushrooms and cook, covered, for 2 hours, or until the chicken is very tender.
7 Serve the chicken with the vegetables, topped with tarragon leaves, if liked.

**Prep + cook time
20 minutes + 6 hours
Serves 6**

BEEF BRISKET & MUSHROOM STEW

1½ tbsp olive oil
1.2kg (2½lb) thick piece of beef brisket, trimmed of fat
2 onions, thinly sliced
4 cloves of garlic, crushed
2½ tbsp Dijon mustard
1½ tbsp instant coffee granules
2½ tbsp Worcestershire sauce
200g (7oz) chestnut mushrooms, sliced
1 litre (4 cups) hot beef stock
35g (¼ cup) cornflour
120g (½ cup) sour cream
salt and freshly ground black pepper

TO SERVE:
mashed potatoes
chopped chives

1 Heat the oil in a large frying pan over high heat. Season the beef, then add to the pan and cook for 3 minutes on each side, or until browned all over. Transfer to a 4.5-litre (5-quart) slow cooker.
2 In the same frying pan, cook the onions, garlic, mustard, and coffee, stirring, for 5 minutes, or until the onions brown. Transfer to the slow cooker, then add the Worcestershire sauce, mushrooms, and stock. Cook, covered, on low for 7 hours or until tender.
3 Carefully remove the beef from the slow cooker and shred it coarsely using two forks. Return it to the slow cooker.
4 Combine the cornflour and sour cream in a small bowl, then stir through the stew.
5 Adjust the slow cooker to high and cook, uncovered, for 10 minutes, or until the sauce boils and thickens. Season to taste.
6 Serve the stew with mashed potatoes, topped with chopped chives.

Prep + cook time
15 minutes + 7 hours
10 minutes
Serves 4

MEATLOAF WITH STICKY TOMATO GLAZE

500g (1lb 2oz) lean minced beef
500g (1lb 2oz) minced pork
1 red onion, coarsely grated
1 carrot, coarsely grated
3 cloves of garlic, crushed
120g (2 cups) fresh breadcrumbs
2 eggs, lightly beaten
2½ tbsp tomato purée
2½ tbsp wholegrain mustard
2½ tbsp Worcestershire sauce
1 tbsp smoked paprika
handful of parsley, finely chopped, plus extra leaves to serve
small handful of oregano leaves, finely chopped
salt and freshly ground black pepper

STICKY TOMATO GLAZE:
400g (14oz) can diced tomatoes
60ml (¼ cup) maple syrup
1 tbsp Worcestershire sauce
2 tsp smoked paprika

TO SERVE:
steamed green beans
grated Parmesan

1 Combine the sticky tomato glaze ingredients in a small bowl and season to taste. Set aside.
2 Remove the pot from a 4.5-litre (5-quart) oval slow cooker. Line the base of the pot with foil, then damp kitchen paper, then an oval of baking paper. Cut two long, wide strips of baking paper, then place in a criss-cross pattern over the base and sides, extending over the top. Return the pot to the slow cooker.
3 Combine the beef, pork, onion, carrot, garlic, breadcrumbs, eggs, tomato purée, mustard, Worcestershire sauce, paprika, chopped herbs, and 60ml (¼ cup) of the glaze in a large bowl, and season.
4 Press the beef mixture onto the base of the slow cooker and top with half the remaining glaze. Cook, covered, on low for 4 hours.
5 Turn the slow cooker off and let it stand for 20 minutes.
6 Preheat the grill to high. Line an oven tray with foil, then brush with oil.
7 Using the baking paper tabs, carefully lift the meatloaf out of the slow cooker onto the prepared tray. Top with the remaining glaze. Place under the grill for 5 minutes, or until the glaze is caramelized.
8 Serve with steamed beans, grated Parmesan, and extra parsley leaves.

TIP Placing the wide strips of baking paper in a criss-cross pattern over the base and up over the sides creates handy tabs that make it easier to lift the meatloaf out of the pot.

Prep + cook time
10 minutes + 4 hours
5 minutes, plus standing
Serves 4–6

CREAMY CHICKEN & CORN MAC 'N' CHEESE WITH PANCETTA CRUMB

---

1 leek, thinly sliced
420g (14½oz) can sweetcorn cream style (see tip)
70g (¼ cup) Dijon mustard
300ml (1¼ cup) single cream
750ml (3 cups) hot vegetable stock
500g (1lb 2oz) boneless chicken thighs
2 corn cobs, kernels cut off
200g (7oz) small pasta shells
180g (1½ cups) grated Cheddar
salt and freshly ground black pepper

PANCETTA CRUMB:
2½ tbsp extra virgin olive oil
100g (3½oz) chopped pancetta
50g (⅔ cup) panko breadcrumbs
1½ tbsp finely chopped chives

TO SERVE (OPTIONAL):
sautéed cavolo nero
herb bread

1 Place the leek, canned corn, mustard, cream, and stock in a 4.5-litre (5-quart) slow cooker and stir to combine. Place the chicken on top and cook, covered, on low for 4 hours, or until the chicken is tender.
2 Remove the chicken from the slow cooker and shred it coarsely using two forks. Return the shredded chicken to the slow cooker, then add the corn kernels and pasta. Season well and stir to combine. Cover the slow cooker with a clean tea towel, place the lid on top, then fold the towel up over the lid. Cook, covered, for 1 hour 30 minutes, or until the pasta is tender and most of the liquid is absorbed, stirring halfway through the cooking time.
3 Turn the slow cooker off. Stir through two-thirds of the cheese. Let it stand, covered, for 10 minutes.
4 Meanwhile, for the pancetta crumb, heat the oil in a large non-stick frying pan over high heat and cook the pancetta, stirring, for 1 minute, or until golden. Add the breadcrumbs and cook, stirring occasionally, for 2 minutes, or until golden. Remove from the heat, stir in the chives, and season
5 Preheat the grill to high.
6 Remove the pot from the slow cooker. Sprinkle the mac 'n' cheese with the remaining grated cheese. Grill for 5 minutes, or until the cheese is golden and melted.
7 Sprinkle the mac 'n' cheese with the pancetta crumb. Serve with sautéed cavolo nero and bread, if liked.

KEEP IT Store in an airtight container for 3 days in the fridge.

TIP Sweetcorn cream style (creamed corn) is available online.

Prep + cook time
10 minutes + 5 hours 40 minutes, plus standing
Serves 4–6

LAMB & CHICKPEA STEW WITH ALMONDS

2½ tbsp olive oil
1kg (2¼lb) lamb shoulder, cut into 4cm (1½-inch) pieces
1 large onion, roughly chopped
2 cloves of garlic, finely chopped
1½ tbsp baharat (see tip)
10 saffron threads
2½ tbsp honey
400g (14oz) can crushed tomatoes
500ml (2 cups) chicken stock
12 pickling onions
400g (14oz) can chickpeas, drained and rinsed
40g (½ cup) flaked almonds, toasted
salt and freshly ground black pepper

TO SERVE:
pearl couscous

1 Preheat a 5-litre (5-quart) slow cooker on high.

2 Heat the oil in a large frying pan over high heat and cook the lamb, in batches, for 3 minutes, or until browned all over. Transfer the lamb to the slow cooker.

3 Add the chopped onion and garlic to the same frying pan and cook, stirring, over medium–high heat for 3 minutes, or until the onion softens. Add the spices and cook, stirring, for 1 minute, or until fragrant. Stir in the honey, canned tomatoes, and stock and bring to the boil.

4 Adjust the slow cooker setting to low and carefully pour the tomato mixture over the lamb in the slow cooker. Cook, covered, for 3 hours.

5 Add the pickling onions to the slow cooker and stir to combine. Cook, covered, for 3 hours 30 minutes, or until the lamb is tender. Stir in the chickpeas and cook, uncovered, for 10 minutes, or until heated through.

6 Sprinkle the almonds over the stew and serve with couscous.

TIP To make your own baharat, combine 1 teaspoon each of ground cumin, turmeric, ginger, and cinnamon.

KEEP IT The stew is suitable to freeze after the chickpeas have been heated.

Prep + cook time
15 minutes + 6 hours 40 minutes
Serves 4–6

CHICKEN & CHORIZO FREGOLA POT

1 orange
1½ tbsp olive oil
8 large chicken drumsticks, about 1.2kg (2½lb)
2 chorizo sausages, thickly sliced
1 onion, finely chopped
1 celery stalk, finely chopped
3 cloves of garlic, thinly sliced
¼ tsp chilli flakes
1½ tbsp tomato purée
1 tomato, finely chopped
pinch of saffron
1 litre (4 cups) chicken stock
250g (9oz) fregola (see tip)
120g (1 cup) frozen peas

TO SERVE (OPTIONAL):
parsley leaves

1 Finely grate the zest from the orange, then squeeze it; you need 1 tablespoon zest and 60ml (¼ cup) juice.

2 Heat the oil in a large frying pan over high heat and cook the chicken, in batches, for 5 minutes, or until browned all over. Transfer to a 5-litre (5-quart) slow cooker.

3 Add the chorizo to the same frying pan and cook, stirring, for 2 minutes until golden. Add the onion, celery, garlic, and chilli flakes and cook, stirring, for a further 3 minutes, or until the vegetables soften. Transfer to the slow cooker, then add the tomato purée, chopped tomato, orange zest and juice, saffron, and stock and stir.

4 Cook, covered, on low for 3 hours.

5 Add the fregola and stir to combine. Cook, covered, for a further 1 hour. Stir in the peas and let stand, uncovered, for 5 minutes, or until heated through.

6 Serve the chicken and fregola sprinkled with parsley leaves, if liked.

TIP Fregola is a Sardinian pasta made from hard durum wheat flour which is rolled, sun-dried, and toasted to a mix of shades of yellow, gold, and brown. It is available from specialist food stores.

Prep + cook time
15 minutes + 4 hours,
plus standing
Serves 4–6

DESSERTS

This chapter is packed full of warming dishes to satisfy a sweet tooth. From poached and baked fruits to comforting creamy puddings, the slow cooker takes a lot of the work out of making indulgent desserts, cakes, buns, and sweet treats.

ORANGE CARAMEL FLAN

200g (1 cup) caster sugar
1 orange, zested into thin strips, plus 1½ tbsp finely grated orange zest (see tips)
6 eggs
600ml (2½ cups) milk
395g (14oz) can sweetened condensed milk

TO SERVE:
toasted flaked almonds
whipped cream

1 Line the base and sides of a 6.5-litre (7-quart) slow cooker pot with four layers of baking paper, placing each layer in opposite directions and partway up the sides.
2 Place the sugar and 125ml (½ cup) water in a small saucepan over medium heat. Stir, without boiling, until the sugar dissolves. Add the orange zest strips and bring to the boil, without stirring. Boil for 10 minutes, or until dark golden brown. Pour the caramel into the lined pot and swirl it around to coat the base. Return the pot to the slow cooker.
3 Meanwhile, whisk the eggs, grated orange zest, and both milks in a large bowl until combined. Stand for 5 minutes.
4 Strain the custard over the caramel in the slow cooker. Cover with a clean tea towel, place the lid on top, then fold the towel over the lid.
5 Cook on low for 3 hours, or until just set (the flan will be slightly wobbly in the centre).
6 Remove the pot. Gently pull the edge of the flan away from the paper with your fingertips — this will prevent the custard from cracking as it cools. Cool to room temperature, then chill overnight to firm up.
7 Using the baking paper, carefully lift the flan out of the pot to a serving platter. Remove the paper. Drizzle with the remaining caramel from the slow cooker pot, sprinkle with almonds, and serve with cream.

TIPS You need to start this recipe 1 day ahead. You need 2 oranges for this recipe: use a zesting tool to create thin strips from one orange, and finely grate the other.

**Prep + cook time 15 minutes + 3 hours, plus overnight chilling
Serves 8**

QUEEN OF PUDDINGS WITH TAPIOCA

---

3 eggs, separated
200g (1 cup) caster sugar
300ml (1¼ cups) milk, warmed
200ml (scant 1 cup) single cream, warmed
75g (1 cup) panko breadcrumbs
50g (¼ cup) tapioca pearls
2 tsp finely grated lemon zest
1 tsp vanilla bean paste
200g (1⅓ cups) frozen mixed berries

1 Preheat a 6.5-litre (7-quart) slow cooker on low heat.
2 Whisk the egg yolks and half the sugar in a large bowl until combined and slightly paler. Gradually whisk in the warmed milk and cream until combined. Stir in the breadcrumbs, tapioca, lemon zest, and vanilla. Divide the mixture amongst four 250ml (1-cup) ramekins or heatproof bowls and spoon the berries on top.
3 Place the ramekins in the slow cooker and pour in enough hot water to come halfway up the sides of the ramekins. Cover the slow cooker with a clean tea towel, place the lid on top, then fold the towel up over the lid. Cook on low for 4 hours, or until set.
4 Turn the slow cooker off and let the puddings cool to room temperature.
5 Whisk the egg whites and remaining sugar in the bowl of an electric mixer until stiff peaks form. Divide among the puddings. Use a kitchen blow torch to lightly brown the meringue.

TIPS Use heatproof dishes that are taller rather than wider, so all four fit within the slow cooker pot – or you could use a larger slow cooker. If you don't have a kitchen blow torch, place the puddings on an oven tray and grill on high until lightly browned.

Prep + cook time
15 minutes + 4 hours
5 minutes
Serves 4

SPICED BAKED APPLES WITH OATS & SKYR

70g (5 tbsp) unsalted butter, melted
75g (⅓ cup) brown sugar
1 tsp ground cinnamon
2 tsp finely grated lemon zest
45g (½ cup) rye flakes (see tips)
35g (¼ cup) oat bran
2½ tbsp raisins
40g (¼ cup) natural almonds, roasted and coarsely chopped
6 large apples, about 1.25kg (2¾lb), cored (see tips)
250ml (1 cup) apple juice
10 cardamom pods, crushed
60ml (¼ cup) whisky
20g (1½ tbsp) unsalted butter

WHIPPED SKYR:
250ml (1 cup) double cream
140g (½ cup) vanilla skyr (see tips)

1 Combine 50g (3½ tbsp) of the butter with the sugar, cinnamon, lemon zest, rye flakes, oat bran, raisins, and almonds in a bowl.

2 Run a small sharp knife around the middle of each apple to lightly score; do not cut under the skin. Spoon 1 tablespoon of the rye flake mixture into the core of each apple, pressing down firmly to compact. Top each apple evenly with another tablespoon of mixture.

3 Pour the apple juice into a 5.5-litre (6-quart) slow cooker, then add the cardamom. Arrange the apples over the base.

4 Cook, covered, on low for 4 hours.

5 Remove the apples from the slow cooker. Strain the cooking liquid into a small saucepan over medium heat and discard the solids.

6 Stir in the whisky, bring to the boil, and cook for 3 minutes, or until slightly reduced. Whisk in the remaining 20g (1½ tbsp) of butter.

7 For the whipped skyr, whisk the cream until soft peaks form, then whisk in the skyr.

8 Serve the apples warm with the whisky sauce and whipped skyr.

TIPS Rye flakes are available from health food stores; rolled oats will work equally well. An apple that holds its shape is best for this recipe. Skyr is an Icelandic yogurt, available from major supermarkets; you can use Greek yogurt instead, if liked.

Prep + cook time
15 minutes + 4 hours
5 minutes
Serves 6

DESSERTS

NEGRONI POACHED QUINCE

200g (1 cup) caster sugar
125ml (½ cup) gin
125ml (½ cup) Campari
125ml (½ cup) vermouth
6 wide strips orange zest
1 cinnamon stick
1 vanilla pod, split lengthways and seeds scraped
3 large quinces

TO SERVE:
crème fraîche
puff pastry finger biscuits

1 Place the sugar, gin, Campari, vermouth, orange zest, cinnamon, scraped vanilla pod and seeds, and 1 litre (4 cups) water in a 6-litre (6½-quart) slow cooker set on low. Stir until the sugar has dissolved.
2 Peel each quince, cut into quarters, and remove the core. Add each quince to the slow cooker immediately to prevent discoloration. Place a piece of baking paper (cut to fit) directly on the quinces. Cook, covered, on low for 6 hours, or until the quinces are soft and rose-coloured.
3 Remove the quinces from the slow cooker with a slotted spoon and pour the poaching liquid into a saucepan. Bring to the boil and cook for 15 minutes, or until the syrup is reduced and slightly thickened.
4 Serve the quinces warm or at room temperature, with crème fraîche, syrup, and puff pastry biscuits.

TIP Use any leftover syrup as a base for a cocktail, or drizzle it over yogurt or ice cream.

**Prep + cook time
15 minutes + 6 hours
15 minutes
Serves 6**

SALTED CARAMEL & SPECULAAS COOKIE BARS

250g (9oz) unsalted butter, softened
100g (½ cup) caster sugar
100g (½ cup) brown sugar
1 tsp ground cinnamon
1 tsp ground ginger
1 tsp mixed spice
¼ tsp ground cardamom
¼ tsp freshly grated nutmeg
1 egg
225g (1½ cups) plain flour
½ tsp baking powder
135g (4oz) packet chewy caramels, chopped
100g (3½oz) dark chocolate (70% cocoa), melted and cooled
sea salt flakes, for sprinkling

1 Lightly grease the pot of a 4.5-litre (5-quart) slow cooker. Line the base of the pot with foil, then damp kitchen paper, then an oval of baking paper. Cut two long, wide strips of baking paper, then place in a criss-cross pattern, over the base and sides, extending over the top of the slow cooker.
2 Beat the butter, sugars, and spices in the bowl of an electric mixer until light and creamy. Beat in the egg until combined. Add the flour and baking powder and beat on low speed until just combined.
3 Press two-thirds of the cookie dough onto the base of the slow cooker pot. (Wrap and chill the remaining dough.) Cook, covered, on low for 1 hour.
4 Sprinkle chopped caramels evenly over the dough in the slow cooker, then crumble the remaining chilled dough over the top.
5 Cover with a clean tea towel, place the lid on top, then fold the towel up over the lid. Cook on low for 2 hours 30 minutes. Turn off, remove the lid and towel, and let it stand for 30 minutes to firm.
6 Using the baking paper tabs, gently lift the cookie out of the slow cooker. Drizzle with melted chocolate and sprinkle with salt. Refrigerate until set. Cut into bars, to serve.

TIPS Placing the wide strips of baking paper in a criss-cross pattern over the base and up over the sides creates handy tabs that make it easier to lift the cookie out of the pot. Adding the damp kitchen paper insulates the cookie, ensuring it doesn't brown and crisp during cooking.

**Prep + cook time
15 minutes + 3 hours 30 minutes, plus standing
Serves 6**

VANILLA, PEACH & COCONUT COBBLER

1.5kg (3¼lb) firm ripe peaches
250g (1¼ cups) caster sugar
1½ tbsp cornflour
2 tsp vanilla bean paste
125g (9 tbsp) unsalted butter, softened
2 eggs
1 cup (150g) self-raising flour, sifted
½ tsp fine sea salt
40g (½ cup) desiccated coconut
125ml (½ cup) milk

TO SERVE:
toasted salted coconut flakes
vanilla ice cream

1 Cut the peaches into 2cm (¾-inch) wedges and arrange on the base of a 4.5-litre (5-quart) slow cooker. Add 100g (½ cup) of the sugar, the cornflour, and vanilla and stir until the peaches are coated.
2 Beat the butter and remaining sugar in a large bowl with an electric mixer until light and fluffy. Beat in the eggs, one at a time, until combined. Add the sifted flour and salt, coconut, and milk and beat until just combined.
3 Spoon the batter over the peaches and spread out until smooth and the fruit is completely covered. Cover the slow cooker with a clean tea towel, place the lid on top, then fold the towel up over the lid.
4 Cook on low for 4 hours, or until the peaches are tender and the cobbler top is light golden.
5 Serve scoops of cobbler with coconut flakes and vanilla ice cream.

**Prep + cook time
15 minutes + 4 hours
Serves 8**

TRES LECHES BRIOCHE PUDDING

1 loaf of brioche, about 400g (14oz), cut into 5cm (2-inch) pieces
1 orange
9 egg yolks
1½ tbsp vanilla bean paste
1 tsp ground cinnamon
1 tsp sea salt flakes
395g (14oz) can sweetened condensed milk
370ml (12½oz) can evaporated milk
250ml (1 cup) whole milk

TO SERVE:
warmed dulce de leche
toasted flaked almonds
single cream

1 Lightly grease the base and side of the pot from a 5.5-litre (6-quart) slow cooker. Line the base and sides with two layers of baking paper. Set the heat to low.
2 Arrange the brioche in the pot in an even layer.
3 Finely grate the zest from the orange. Remove the white pith, then cut the orange into rounds. Cover and set aside until ready to serve.
4 Whisk the egg yolks, vanilla, grated orange zest, cinnamon, salt flakes, and all three milks in a large bowl until smooth. Pour over the brioche in the slow cooker. Gently push the brioche into the custard mixture until evenly soaked.
5 Cover the slow cooker with a clean tea towel, place the lid on top, then fold the towel up over the lid. Cook on low for 3 hours.
6 Remove the pot from the slow cooker and let it stand, covered, for 1 hour.
7 Using the baking paper, carefully lift the pudding out of the pot and peel away the paper.
8 Serve topped with dulce de leche, the orange slices, flaked almonds, and cream for pouring.

Prep + cook time
15 minutes + 3 hours,
plus standing
Serves 6

ESPRESSO CHOC DATE PUDDING

225g (1½ cups) chopped pitted dried dates
165g (¾ cup) brown sugar
60g (4 tbsp) unsalted butter, chopped
180ml (¾ cup) boiling water
1½ tbsp instant espresso coffee granules
35g (⅓ cup) cocoa powder, sifted
1 tsp bicarbonate of soda
2 eggs
150g (1 cup) self-raising flour, sifted

ESPRESSO TOFFEE SAUCE:
180ml (¾ cup) single cream
1 tsp instant espresso coffee granules
150g (⅔ cup) firmly packed brown sugar
100g (3½oz) unsalted butter, chopped

TO SERVE:
icing sugar
double cream

1 Place the dates, sugar, butter, and boiling water in a saucepan over medium heat and stir until the sugar dissolves. Bring to the boil, then cook for 1 minute. Remove the pan from the heat. Add the coffee granules and sifted cocoa and stir until dissolved. Let it stand for 5 minutes to cool. Stir in the bicarbonate of soda, then stir in the eggs and flour until well combined.
2 Meanwhile, grease a 2-litre (8-cup), 18cm (7¼-inch) round pudding basin with a lid and line the base with a round of baking paper.
3 Spoon the pudding mixture into the basin, cover tightly with foil and add the lid. Place the basin in the pot of a 4.5-litre (5-quart) slow cooker and pour in enough boiling water to come halfway up the side of the basin.
4 Cook, covered, on low for 4 hours 30 minutes, or until crumbs cling to a skewer when inserted.
5 Remove the basin from the slow cooker. Stand for 15 minutes before turning out onto a serving plate.
6 For the espresso toffee sauce, stir the cream and coffee granules in a saucepan over medium heat until the coffee dissolves. Add the sugar and butter and stir, without boiling, until the sugar dissolves. Bring to the boil, then reduce the heat to low and simmer, uncovered, for 2 minutes, or until thickened slightly.
7 Dust the pudding with icing sugar, cut into slices, and serve with cream and the warm sauce.

Prep + cook time
15 minutes + 4 hours
30 minutes, plus standing
Serves 8

MANDARIN & EARL GREY TEA BUNS WITH BURNT BUTTER ICING

375g (2½ cups) bread flour, sifted
1¾ tsp dried yeast
2½ tbsp caster sugar
1½ tbsp Earl Grey tea leaves
½ tsp baking powder
¼ tsp fine sea salt
1½ tbsp honey
60ml (¼ cup) light flavoured olive oil
1½ tbsp finely grated mandarin zest, plus extra to serve

BURNT BUTTER ICING:
50g (3½ tbsp) butter, chopped
160g (1 cup) icing sugar, sifted
60ml (¼ cup) mandarin juice

TO SERVE:
softened butter

1 Combine the flour, yeast, sugar, tea leaves, baking powder, and salt in the bowl of an electric mixer fitted with a dough hook.
2 Combine the honey, oil, mandarin zest, and 250ml (1 cup) water in a small jug and add to the flour mixture. Mix on medium speed until the dough is smooth and elastic.
3 Divide the dough into six portions and roll into balls.
4 Pour 125ml (½ cup) water into the pot of a 4.5-litre (5-quart) slow cooker. Place a metal rack covered in foil onto the base. Line with three layers of baking paper, allowing it to come up the sides.
5 Arrange the dough balls in the slow cooker. Cover with a clean tea towel, set the slow cooker to low, and let it prove for 45 minutes.
6 Place the lid on the slow cooker, then fold the towel up over the lid. Cook on low for 2 hours 30 minutes.
7 Turn the slow cooker off and leave to stand for 30 minutes. Remove the lid and towel and let it cool completely.
8 Meanwhile, make burnt butter icing. Cook the butter in a small saucepan over medium–high heat for 3 minutes, or until beginning to brown. Transfer to a bowl and whisk in the sifted icing sugar and mandarin juice until combined.
9 Drizzle the buns with the icing, sprinkle with extra mandarin zest, and serve with softened butter.

Prep + cook time
15 minutes + 3 hours
15 minutes, plus standing
Serves 6

COCONUT RICE PUDDING WITH PASSION FRUIT SALTED CARAMEL

200g (7oz) arborio rice
600ml (2½ cups) coconut milk
300ml (1¼ cups) whole milk
300ml (1¼ cups) single cream
50g (¼ cup) caster sugar
50g (¼ cup) coconut sugar
1 star anise
2 makrut lime leaves
½ pineapple, peeled, cored, and sliced
1 mango, sliced

PASSION FRUIT SALTED CARAMEL:
100g (1 cup) caster sugar
170g (5½oz) canned passion fruit
½ tsp sea salt flakes
2 tsp finely grated lime zest
1 tbsp lime juice

TO SERVE:
Greek yogurt
mint leaves

1 Combine the rice, milks, cream, sugars, star anise, and lime leaves in a 5.5-litre (6-quart) slow cooker. Cook, covered, on low, for 4 hours.

2 Remove the star anise and leaves. Turn the slow cooker off and let it cool to room temperature.

3 Meanwhile, for the passion fruit salted caramel, place the sugar in an even layer in a large frying pan over medium–high heat. Gently swirl the pan occasionally for 4 minutes, or until the sugar dissolves and turns an amber colour. Carefully stir in the passion fruit, salt flakes, and 60ml (¼ cup) water (the mixture will bubble and the sugar will harden). Cook, stirring, for 2 minutes, or until the sugar dissolves. Remove from the heat. Stir in the lime zest and juice. Refrigerate for 2 hours, or until chilled.

4 Spoon the rice pudding into serving bowls and top with the pineapple and mango. Drizzle with the caramel and serve topped with yogurt and mint.

Prep + cook time
15 minutes + 4 hours
Serves 4

RHUBARB SPOON CAKE

500g (1lb 2oz) rhubarb, cut into 4cm (1½-inch) lengths
165g (¾ cup) demerara sugar, plus extra for sprinkling
2½ tbsp orange juice
200g (1⅓ cups) plain flour
80g (½ cup) ground almonds
2 tsp baking powder
½ tsp bicarbonate of soda
150g (¾ cup) brown sugar
175g (1½ sticks) unsalted butter, melted
2 eggs
1½ tbsp finely grated orange zest
150ml (⅔ cup) milk
1 tsp vanilla extract
25g (⅓ cup) flaked almonds

TO SERVE:
cream or custard

1 Lightly grease the pot of a 5.5-litre (6-quart) slow cooker, then line the base and sides with a layer of foil and a layer of baking paper.
2 Combine the rhubarb, demerara sugar, and orange juice in a bowl. Set aside.
3 Combine the flour, ground almonds, baking powder, bicarbonate of soda, and brown sugar in a large bowl.
4 Whisk the melted butter, eggs, orange zest, milk, and vanilla in a large jug. Pour into the flour mixture and stir to combine.
5 Pour half the batter into the slow cooker and top evenly with the rhubarb mixture. Pour over the remaining batter. Sprinkle evenly with the flaked almonds and extra demerara sugar.
6 Cover the slow cooker with a clean tea towel and place the lid on top, then fold the towel up over the lid. Cook on low for 3 hours.
7 Turn the slow cooker off and let it stand for 1 hour.
8 Preheat the grill to high. Place the slow cooker pot under the grill for 5 minutes, or until the top of the cake is golden.
9 Serve the cake with cream or custard.

Prep + cook time
15 minutes + 3 hours
5 minutes, plus standing
Serves 6

CHOCOLATE HAZELNUT CHEESECAKE

250g (9oz) chocolate sandwich biscuits
80g (2¾oz) butter, melted
500g (1lb 2oz) cream cheese, softened
½ cup (110g) caster sugar
750g jar hazelnut chocolate spread
3 eggs
2 tbsp skinless roasted hazelnuts, coarsely chopped

1 Grease a 20cm (8in) round springform tin; line bottom and side with baking parchment. Make sure the tin fits in the slow cooker without touching the side; remove the tin. Place a wire rack in the slow cooker.
2 Process the biscuits to fine crumbs; add the butter and process until combined. Press the mixture into the bottom of the lined tin and smooth the surface with a spoon. Place in the freezer for 5 minutes while preparing the filling.
3 Process the cream cheese and sugar in a clean food processor until smooth and combined. Add 1½ cups (500g) of the hazelnut chocolate spread and process until combined. With the motor running, add 1 egg at a time, processing until combined.
4 Add 1 cup (250ml) water to the slow cooker. Pour the filling mixture over the biscuit base in the tin. Taking care, place the tin on the rack in the slow cooker.
5 Cover with a clean tea towel, then cover with the slow cooker lid, then fold the tea towel up over the lid. Cook on a high heat for 2 hours.
6 Turn the slow cooker off and allow the cheesecake to stand inside the covered cooker for 1 hour. Remove the tin and allow to stand for 30 minutes. Refrigerate for 4 hours or until cold.
7 Just before serving, combine the remaining chocolate spread with a little boiling water in a heatproof bowl; whisk until smooth. Serve the cheesecake topped with the sauce and hazelnuts.

**Prep + cook time
30 mins, plus standing and refrigeration + 2 hours
Serves 10**

INDEX

Page numbers in **bold** refer to illustrations.

A

almonds
  almond romesco **96**, 97
  lamb & chickpea stew with almonds 142, **143**
  spiced almond chicken rice **52**, 53
apples
  chicken, leek & cider casserole 22, **23**
  pork, apple & fennel stew **120**, 121
  spiced baked apples with oats & skyr 152, **153**
aubergines
  aubergine dal with rainbow chard 58, **59**
  caponata-inspired pork **92**, 93
  upside-down lamb rice **88**, 89

B

bacon, cheese & sour cream jacket potatoes 36, **37**
bao, beef short rib 32, **33**
beans
  beef shin, beetroot & pomegranate soup 90, **91**
  chipotle bean tacos **16**, 17
  chorizo, potato & white bean stew **96**, 97
beef
  beef brisket & mushroom stew **136**, 137
  beef, coconut & peanut curry **70**, 71
  beef ragù with torn pasta sheets 44, **45**
  beef shin, beetroot & pomegranate soup 90, **91**
  beef short rib bao 32, **33**
  five-spice braised salt beef 122, **123**
  green curry beef ribs **64**, 65
  Japanese beef curry **74**, 75
  meatloaf with sticky tomato glaze 138, **139**
  Penang beef curry 54, **55**
  red wine-braised beef ribs with mushrooms **104**, 105
  shredded beef & mushroom pot pies 126, **127**
  sumac & onion-braised beef cheeks 108, **109**

beetroot
  beef shin, beetroot & pomegranate soup 90, **91**
  confit chicken & root vegetables 86, **87**
  lamb shank & beetroot curry **78**, 79
berries: queen of puddings with tapioca **150**, 151
bistro side salad 11
black beans: chipotle bean tacos **16**, 17
bread
  beef short rib bao 32, **33**
  cheese toasts 22, **23**
  cheesy pull-apart rolls 11
  courgette & chorizo cornbread slice 130, **131**
  mojo pork rolls 112, **113**
brioche pudding, tres leches 160, **161**
buns, mandarin & Earl Grey tea 164, **165**
butternut squash
  butternut squash & goat's cheese barley risotto **28**, 29
  butternut squash & tomato curry **56**, 57

C

cabbage
  cabbage with coriander chutney 62, **63**
  pickled cabbage **16**, 17
cake, rhubarb spoon 168, **169**
Campari: Negroni poached quince **154**, 155
capers: caponata-inspired pork **92**, 93
caramel
  coconut rice pudding with passion fruit salted caramel **166**, 167
  orange caramel flan 148, **149**
  salted caramel & speculaas cookie bars 156, **157**
cashew & cauliflower curry **82**, 83
casseroles *see* stews and casseroles
cauliflower
  cashew & cauliflower curry **82**, 83
  'roast' chicken korma with coconut rice stuffing & cauliflower 76, **77**
cavolo nero
  chorizo, potato & white bean stew **96**, 97
  honey-glazed greens 11
celeriac: braised duck legs with juniper & thyme **106**, 107

cheese
  bacon, cheese & sour cream jacket potatoes 36, **37**
  beef ragù with torn pasta sheets, 44, **45**
  braised lamb shanks with beans & feta **128**, 129
  butternut squash & goat's cheese barley risotto **28**, 29
  cheese toasts 22, **23**
  cheesy pull-apart rolls 11
  chipotle bean tacos **16**, 17
  creamy chicken & corn mac 'n' cheese with pancetta crumb **140**, 141
  deep-pan pepperoni pizza **46**, 47
  lamb chops & brown rice pilaf **30**, 31
  mojo pork rolls 112, **113**
  slow cooker pastitsio 118, **119**
chicken
  chicken & chorizo fregola pot **144**, 145
  chicken & coconut laksa **60**, 61
  chicken laksa curry 80, **81**
  chicken, leek & cider casserole 22, **23**
  'clay pot' chicken rice **114**, 115
  confit chicken & root vegetables 86, **87**
  creamy chicken & corn mac 'n' cheese with pancetta crumb **140**, 141
  crispy chilli peanut chicken 26, **27**
  French-style chicken legs 134, **135**
  milk-poached whole chicken 94, **95**
  'roast' chicken korma with coconut rice stuffing & cauliflower 76, **77**
  spiced almond chicken rice **52**, 53
  spicy upside-down pineapple chicken 18, **19**
  sweet & salty chicken wings **42**, 43
  Thai coconut & chicken soup 50, **51**
chickpeas: lamb & chickpea stew with almonds 142, **143**
chillies
  beef, coconut & peanut curry **70**, 71
  braised pork with pineapple & sweet chilli **34**, 35
  chicken & coconut laksa **60**, 61
  crispy chilli peanut chicken 26, **27**
  spicy upside-down pineapple chicken 18, **19**
chipotle bean tacos **16**, 17

172

INDEX

chocolate
    espresso choc date pudding 162, **163**
    hazelnut cheesecake **170**, 171
    salted caramel & speculaas cookie bars 156, **157**
chorizo
    chicken & chorizo fregola pot **144**, 145
    chorizo, potato & white bean stew **96**, 97
    courgette & chorizo cornbread slice 130, **131**
choy sum: chicken & coconut laksa **60**, 61
chutney, coriander 62, **63**
cider: chicken, leek & cider casserole 22, **23**
'clay pot' chicken rice **114**, 115
cobbler, vanilla, peach & coconut **158**, 159
coconut, desiccated
    beef, coconut & peanut curry **70**, 71
    vanilla, peach & coconut cobbler **158**, 159
coconut, shredded: 'roast' chicken korma with coconut rice stuffing & cauliflower 76, **77**
coconut cream
    cashew & cauliflower curry **82**, 83
    chicken laksa curry 80, **81**
    green curry beef ribs **64**, 65
coconut milk
    aubergine dal with rainbow chard 58, **59**
    chicken & coconut laksa **60**, 61
    coconut rice pudding with passion fruit salted caramel **166**, 167
    Penang beef curry 54, **55**
    prawn & squid coconut hot pot 66, **67**
    'roast' chicken korma with coconut rice stuffing & cauliflower 76, **77**
    Thai coconut & chicken soup 50, **51**
coffee: espresso choc date pudding 162, **163**
coleslaw: sweet & salty chicken wings **42**, 43
condensed milk
    orange caramel flan 148, **149**
    tres leches brioche pudding 160, **161**
confit chicken & root vegetables 86, **87**
cookie bars, salted caramel & speculaas 156, **157**
coriander chutney 62, **63**
corn: creamy chicken & corn mac 'n' cheese with pancetta crumb **140**, 141

cornbread slice, courgette & chorizo 130, **131**
crispy chilli peanut chicken 26, **27**
cucumber, pickled 32, **33**
currants: lamb chops & brown rice pilaf **30**, 31
curry
    beef, coconut & peanut curry **70**, 71
    butternut squash & tomato curry **56**, 57
    cashew & cauliflower curry **82**, 83
    chicken laksa curry 80, **81**
    green curry beef ribs **64**, 65
    Japanese beef curry **74**, 75
    lamb shank & beetroot curry **78**, 79
    Penang beef curry 54, **55**
    'roast' chicken korma with coconut rice stuffing & cauliflower 76, **77**
    spiced yogurt lamb curry 72, **73**
    Thai coconut & chicken soup 50, **51**
    whole lamb shoulder rogan josh **68**, 69

D

dal: aubergine dal with rainbow chard 58, **59**
dates: espresso choc date pudding 162, **163**
dressing, herb **24**, 25
duck: braised duck legs with juniper & thyme **106**, 107

E

Earl Grey tea: mandarin & Earl Grey tea buns 164, **165**
eggs
    courgette & chorizo cornbread slice 130, **131**
    herb & walnut frittata 40, **41**
    orange caramel flan 148, **149**
    queen of puddings with tapioca **150**, 151
    tres leches brioche pudding 160, **161**
espresso choc date pudding 162, **163**
evaporated milk: tres leches brioche pudding 160, **161**

F

fennel
    lamb neck with rosemary & preserved lemon 98, **99**
    pork, apple & fennel stew **120**, 121
figs: honey balsamic pork belly **100**, 101

fish: salt 'baked' trout with herby potatoes 102, **103**
five-spice braised salt beef 122, **123**
flan, orange caramel 148, **149**
fregola: chicken & chorizo fregola pot **144**, 145
French-style chicken legs 134, **135**
frittata, herb & walnut 40, **41**

G

garlic yogurt **132**, 133
gin: Negroni poached quince **154**, 155
green beans
    braised lamb shanks with beans & feta **128**, 129
    braised pork with pineapple & sweet chilli **34**, 35
    honey balsamic pork belly **100**, 101
green curry beef ribs **64**, 65
greens, honey-glazed 11

H

ham: mojo pork rolls 112, **113**
herbs
    herb & walnut frittata 40, **41**
    herb dressing **24**, 25
    herby lemon lamb shoulder **24**, 25
    salt 'baked' trout with herby potatoes 102, **103**
honey
    crispy chilli peanut chicken 26, **27**
    honey balsamic pork belly **100**, 101
    honey-glazed greens 11
hot pot, prawn & squid coconut 66, **67**
hummus: sumac & onion-braised beef cheeks 108, **109**

J

jacket potatoes, bacon, cheese & sour cream 36, **37**
Japanese beef curry **74**, 75
juniper: braised duck legs with juniper & thyme **106**, 107

K

kale
    butternut squash & tomato curry **56**, 57
    honey-glazed greens 11
    pork, barley & kale stew **124**, 125
korma: 'roast' chicken korma with coconut rice stuffing & cauliflower 76, **77**

173

INDEX

L

laksa
  chicken & coconut laksa **60**, 61
  chicken laksa curry 80, **81**
lamb
  braised lamb shanks with beans & feta **128**, 129
  herby lemon lamb shoulder **24**, 25
  lamb & chickpea stew with almonds 142, **143**
  lamb chops & brown rice pilaf **30**, 31
  lamb neck with rosemary & preserved lemon 98, **99**
  lamb shank & beetroot curry **78**, 79
  slow cooker pastitsio 118, **119**
  spiced yogurt lamb curry 72, **73**
  upside-down lamb rice **88**, 89
  whole lamb shoulder rogan josh **68**, 69
leeks: chicken, leek & cider casserole 22, **23**
lemons: herby lemon lamb shoulder **24**, 25
lemons, preserved: lamb neck with rosemary & preserved lemon 98, **99**
lentils
  aubergine dal with rainbow chard 58, **59**
  mixed mushroom & lentil ragù **20**, 21
  sweet potato, turmeric & lentil soup **38**, 39
lettuce: slow-cooked pork lettuce wraps **110**, 111

M

mandarin & Earl Grey tea buns with burnt butter icing 164, **165**
mango: coconut rice pudding with passion fruit salted caramel **166**, 167
meatloaf with sticky tomato glaze 138, **139**
milk
  milk-poached whole chicken 94, **95**
  tres leches brioche pudding 160, **161**
mojo pork rolls 112, **113**
mushrooms
  beef brisket & mushroom stew **136**, 137
  'clay pot' chicken rice **114**, 115
  deep-pan pepperoni pizza **46**, 47
  French-style chicken legs 134, **135**
  mixed mushroom & lentil ragù **20**, 21
  red wine-braised beef ribs with mushrooms **104**, 105

shredded beef & mushroom pot pies 126, **127**
smoky mushroom soup with garlic yogurt **132**, 133
Thai coconut & chicken soup 50, **51**

N

Negroni poached quince **154**, 155
noodles: chicken & coconut laksa **60**, 61

O

oats: spiced baked apples with oats & skyr 152, **153**
olives: caponata-inspired pork **92**, 93
onions
  pickled onion **30**, 31
  sumac & onion-braised beef cheeks 108, **109**
orange caramel flan 148, **149**

P

pak choi
  five-spice braised salt beef 122, **123**
  green curry beef ribs **64**, 65
pancetta
  creamy chicken & corn mac 'n' cheese with pancetta crumb **140**, 141
  red wine-braised beef ribs with mushrooms **104**, 105
passion fruit: coconut rice pudding with passion fruit salted caramel **166**, 167
pasta
  beef ragù with torn pasta sheets 44, **45**
  chicken & chorizo fregola pot **144**, 145
  creamy chicken & corn mac 'n' cheese with pancetta crumb **140**, 141
  slow cooker pastitsio 118, **119**
peaches: vanilla, peach & coconut cobbler **158**, 159
peanut chilli oil: crispy chilli peanut chicken 26, **27**
peanuts
  beef, coconut & peanut curry **70**, 71
  Penang beef curry 54, **55**
pearl barley
  butternut squash & goat's cheese barley risotto **28**, 29
  pork, barley & kale stew **124**, 125
peas: chicken & chorizo fregola pot **144**, 145

Penang beef curry 54, **55**
pepperoni: deep-pan pepperoni pizza **46**, 47
peppers: almond romesco **96**, 97
pickles
  pickled cabbage **16**, 17
  pickled cucumber 32, **33**
  pickled onion **30**, 31
  pickled radish **74**, 75
pies, shredded beef & mushroom pot 126, **127**
pilaf, lamb chops & brown rice **30**, 31
pineapple
  braised pork with pineapple & sweet chilli **34**, 35
  coconut rice pudding with passion fruit salted caramel **166**, 167
  spicy upside-down pineapple chicken 18, **19**
pizza, deep-pan pepperoni **6**, 47
pomegranate juice: beef shin, beetroot & pomegranate soup 90, **91**
pork
  braised pork with pineapple & sweet chilli **34**, 35
  caponata-inspired pork **92**, 93
  honey balsamic pork belly **100**, 101
  meatloaf with sticky tomato glaze 138, **139**
  mojo pork rolls 112, **113**
  pork, apple & fennel stew **120**, 121
  pork, barley & kale stew **124**, 125
  slow-cooked pork lettuce wraps **110**, 111
potatoes
  bacon, cheese & sour cream jacket potatoes 36, **37**
  chicken laksa curry 80, **81**
  chorizo, potato & white bean stew **96**, 97
  herby lemon lamb shoulder **24**, 25
  Japanese beef curry **74**, 75
  pork, barley & kale stew **124**, 125
  prosciutto crumb mash 11
  salt 'baked' trout with herby potatoes 102, **103**
  spiced yogurt lamb curry 72, **73**
prawn & squid coconut hot pot 66, **67**
prosciutto crumb mash 11
puff pastry: shredded beef & mushroom pot pies 126, **127**

Q

queen of puddings with tapioca **150**, 151
quince, Negroni poached **154**, 155

INDEX

R

radicchio
  confit chicken & root vegetables 86, **87**
  honey balsamic pork belly **100**, 101
radish, pickled **74**, 75
ragù
  beef ragù with torn pasta sheets 44, **45**
  mixed mushroom & lentil ragù **20**, 21
  whole sausage & rosemary ragù 14, **15**
rainbow chard, aubergine dal with 58, **59**
raisins: spiced baked apples with oats & skyr 152, **153**
rhubarb spoon cake 168, **169**
rice
  'clay pot' chicken rice **114**, 115
  coconut rice pudding with passion fruit salted caramel **166**, 167
  lamb chops & brown rice pilaf **30**, 31
  'roast' chicken korma with coconut rice stuffing & cauliflower 76, **77**
  spiced almond chicken rice **52**, 53
  spicy upside-down pineapple chicken 18, **19**
  upside-down lamb rice **88**, 89
ricotta: slow cooker pastitsio 118, **119**
risotto, butternut squash & goat's cheese barley **28**, 29
rocket: bistro side salad 11
rogan josh, whole lamb shoulder **68**, 69
romesco, almond **96**, 97
rosemary
  lamb neck with rosemary & preserved lemon 98, **99**
  whole sausage & rosemary ragù 14, **15**

S

salad, bistro side 11
salt 'baked' trout with herby potatoes 102, **103**
salt beef, five-spice braised 122, **123**
salted caramel & speculaas cookie bars 156, **157**
sausages
  whole sausage & rosemary ragù 14, **15**
  see also chorizo
sesame spinach **74**, 75
skyr, spiced baked apples with oats & 152, **153**

slow cooker tips 7–8
soups
  beef shin, beetroot & pomegranate soup 90, **91**
  chicken & coconut laksa **60**, 61
  smoky mushroom soup **132**, 133
  sweet potato, turmeric & lentil soup **38**, 39
  Thai coconut & chicken soup 50, **51**
sour cream: bacon, cheese & sour cream jacket potatoes 36, **37**
speck
  beef shin, beetroot & pomegranate soup 90, **91**
  French-style chicken legs 134, **135**
speculaas cookie bars, salted caramel & 156, **157**
spiced almond chicken rice **52**, 53
spiced baked apples with oats & skyr 152, **153**
spiced yogurt lamb curry 72, **73**
spicy upside-down pineapple chicken 18, **19**
spinach
  herb & walnut frittata 40, **41**
  sesame spinach **74**, 75
squid: prawn & squid coconut hot pot 66, **67**
stews and casseroles
  beef brisket & mushroom stew **136**, 137
  chicken, leek & cider casserole 22, **23**
  chorizo, potato & white bean stew **96**, 97
  lamb & chickpea stew with almonds 142, **143**
  pork, apple & fennel stew **120**, 121
  pork, barley & kale stew **124**, 125
sumac & onion-braised beef cheeks 108, **109**
sweet & salty chicken wings **42**, 43
sweet chilli sauce, braised pork with pineapple & **34**, 35
sweet potato, turmeric & lentil soup **38**, 39

T

tacos, chipotle bean **16**, 17
tapioca, queen of puddings with **150**, 151
Thai coconut & chicken soup 50, **51**
thyme, braised duck legs with juniper & **106**, 107
toffee: espresso toffee sauce 162, **163**

tomatoes
  beef ragù with torn pasta sheets 44, **45**
  bistro side salad 11
  braised lamb shanks with beans & feta **128**, 129
  butternut squash & tomato curry **56**, 57
  caponata-inspired pork **92**, 93
  cashew & cauliflower curry **82**, 83
  lamb & chickpea stew with almonds 142, **143**
  lamb shank & beetroot curry **78**, 79
  mixed mushroom & lentil ragù **20**, 21
  slow cooker pastitsio 118, **119**
  sticky tomato glaze 138, **139**
  sumac & onion-braised beef cheeks 108, **109**
  whole lamb shoulder rogan josh **68**, 69
  whole sausage & rosemary ragù 14, **15**
tortillas: chipotle bean tacos **16**, 17
tres leches brioche pudding 160, **161**
trout: salt 'baked' trout with herby potatoes 102, **103**
turmeric: sweet potato, turmeric & lentil soup **38**, 39

U

upside-down lamb rice **88**, 89

V

vanilla, peach & coconut cobbler **158**, 159
vegetables, confit chicken & root 86, **87**
vermouth: Negroni poached quince **154**, 155

W

walnuts: herb & walnut frittata 40, **41**
watercress: salt 'baked' trout with herby potatoes 102, **103**
white beans: chorizo, potato & white bean stew **96**, 97
wine: red wine-braised beef ribs with mushrooms **104**, 105
wraps, slow-cooked pork lettuce **110**, 111

Y

yogurt
  garlic yogurt **132**, 133
  spiced yogurt lamb curry 72, **73**

DK LONDON
Editorial Director Cara Armstrong
Senior Editor Lucy Sienkowska
Design Manager Tania Gomes
Production Editor David Almond
Senior Production Controller Samantha Cross
DTP and Design Coordinator Heather Blagden
Sales Material and Jackets Coordinator Emily Cannings
Publishing Director Stephanie Jackson
Art Director Maxine Pedliham

DK DELHI
Project Editor Ankita Gupta
Art Editor Rajoshi Chakraborty
Senior Art Editor Ira Sharma
Managing Art Editor Neha Ahuja Chowdhry
Pre-Production Designer Satish Chandra Gaur
Pre-Production Coordinator Pushpak Tyagi
Pre-Production Manager Balwant Singh
Creative Head Malavika Talukder

First published in Great Britain in 2025 by
Dorling Kindersley Limited
20 Vauxhall Bridge Road,
London SW1V 2SA

The authorised representative in the EEA is
Dorling Kindersley Verlag GmbH. Arnulfstr. 124,
80636 Munich, Germany

Copyright © 2025 Dorling Kindersley Limited
A Penguin Random House Company
10 9 8 7 6 5 4 3 2 1
001–355997–Oct/2025

All rights reserved.
No part of this publication may be reproduced, stored
in or introduced into a retrieval system, or transmitted,
in any form, or by any means (electronic, mechanical,
photocopying, recording, or otherwise), without the
prior written permission of the copyright owner.
DK values and supports copyright. Thank you for respecting
intellectual property laws by not reproducing, scanning
or distributing any part of this publication by any means without
permission. By purchasing an authorised edition,
you are supporting writers and artists and enabling DK to continue
to publish books that inform and inspire readers.
No part of this publication may be used or reproduced in
any manner for the purpose of training artificial intelligence
technologies or systems. In accordance with Article 4(3)
of the DSM Directive 2019/790, DK expressly reserves
this work from the text and data mining exception.

A CIP catalogue record for this book
is available from the British Library.
ISBN: 978-0-2417-8893-6

Printed in Slovakia

www.dk.com

This book was made with Forest
Stewardship Council™ certified
paper – one small step in DK's
commitment to a sustainable future.
Learn more at www.dk.com/uk/
information/sustainability